A SURVIVAL GUIDE FOR WRITERS

John Pilkington was born in Lancashire and held a variety of jobs before discovering that he was a writer. In the 1980s he gave up full-time employment to take a degree in Drama and English, going on to complete his MA at the University of London. He has been writing for over twenty years and has had poetry, stories and many plays broadcast on BBC Radio and on overseas radio, as well as three plays produced in the theatre and a novel published. He has also taught writing courses in London and the West Country and is a former regional chair of the Writers' Guild of Great Britain. He lives in Devon with his partner and son.

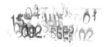 

A SURVIVAL GUIDE
FOR WRITERS

John Pilkington

ROBERT HALE · LONDON

Typeset by
Derek Doyle & Associates, Liverpool.
Printed and bound by
Gutenberg Press Limited, Malta

Contents

Preface

A writer's life is a journey which, once begun, usually continues until death. Even when you are not writing, you are still on the path. Along the way, as with most lives, there are delights as well as disasters. For many writers, perhaps the majority, the journey is an uphill struggle, at least in its early stages and frequently in later ones as well.

Most writers, I have learned, go through bad patches, sometimes severe ones, sometimes for many years. They may be experiencing rejection after rejection; they may find their usual outlets or markets disappearing; they may not even be able, for one reason or another, to write at all. At such times it is very hard to answer those people who, in all innocence, ask the question 'What do you do?' with the words 'I'm a writer'. Polite enquiries usually follow: 'What sort of writing do you do?'; 'What are you working on at the moment?'; and, most depressing of all, 'What have you had published (or performed, or broadcast) recently?' The hapless writer often finds himself or herself making a feeble excuse, or mumbling something incoherent before heading smartly towards the drinks table.

It took me a long time to accept the fact that I was, and probably still am, unlikely to make a fortune from writing. In fact, few writers do, despite popular views to the contrary. With talent and application, however, and a pinch of luck, one can perhaps make a living from it. And there is one singular advantage to being a writer: it is one of the very few professions in which it is possible to turn one's misfortunes to one's advantage. You may, for example, 'write them out', disguised as fiction of one sort or another – or you can simply write about them.

That is how this book came to be written. It is neither a writers' handbook nor a how-to-write book – numerous examples of those exist already. It is a self-help manual for writers – new and not-so-new – in any medium, who are committed to their craft, and is designed to help them negotiate the hazards and pitfalls of the writing profession. Like all true survival guides it is based on solid, first-hand experience. To my fellow scribes, indeed all those who toil at the glowing screen or the blank page, it is affectionately dedicated.

1

Time and Money

If, as Samuel Johnson declared, 'No man but a blockhead ever wrote except for money', that is seldom the reason why writers begin writing. The profession, it is sometimes said, chooses you, or as the novelist John Wain put it: 'Being a writer isn't a profession – it's a condition.' Woody Allen told in an interview how he believed that writers and artists were born with talent, or at least developed it at a very early age, and described a school classmate of his who could draw beautifully and effortlessly. To him, Allen said, it was nothing. The boy did not understand why everyone couldn't simply take up pencil and paper and draw like he could.

If you are lucky, you may find out you are a writer early on, but many, myself included, don't, and waste a lot of time in other areas of endeavour, continually dissatisfied without ever really knowing why. When you finally begin to write, the revelation that this is what you should be doing can be a joy; it can also be rather frightening, leading to all sorts of difficulties, not least of which is, how do you begin to support yourself financially, and still leave time to write? This chapter attempts to address that very basic question, though it must be said at the outset that if there are any easy solutions to the problem apart from winning a large sum on the National Lottery, I have yet to discover them.

Most writers of my acquaintance are frequently short of money, some of them permanently so. I know only two writers of what one might call international standing. One of them supplements his income by means of a university post; the other lives modestly, claiming that he does not earn a huge amount (which I believe is true). Of course, we have all read of famous novelists receiving six-figure advances for their next book, or selling the screen rights for millions; the truth is that such fees are earned by only a tiny percentage of the profession (those people, I hardly need add, will not require this book). Admittedly, as in any area of the arts, luck plays an important role: talent alone is seldom enough. However, there are things that you, the writer, can do to help yourself. The first of these is to be honest with yourself. If you are determined to try and write for your living, or even part of your living, face the fact that success is not likely to be around the next corner; indeed, it may never arrive. And while you pursue your goals and develop your skills, you will need money to live on.

The days of the truly Bohemian writers and artists are, alas, long gone. Between the wars and earlier, it was possible to live in one's garrett on next to nothing, if you didn't mind the physical discomfort, and spend years working on your great novel, or so the cliché goes. How many people really lived like that and how many of them produced lasting works of literature will never be known, but it may be relatively few. By all means, if you haven't done so already, read Ernest Hemingway's *A Moveable Feast* for an account of how a young writer was able to exist very cheaply in Paris in the 1920s, writing fiction on the proceeds of a small journalistic wage. But it may also be worth remembering that Gustave Flaubert, the 'writer's writer', with a vitriolic contempt for the bourgeoisie, wrote his masterpieces while enjoying the security of a private income. Even writers need to eat and wear clothes, and, as writers everywhere continue to eschew Philip Larkin's advice not to have children, so do their families. Larkin himself, as is well known, remained steadily employed as a university librarian throughout his career as a poet, while James Joyce had three children, wrote *Ulysses*, and supported his family by teaching before his writing brought him the success he deserved.

I hope it is becoming clear by now that there are no hard and fast rules; every writer's story is different, as are the means by which they manage to practise their craft. We come to writing at various times in our lives, and by various routes, and we are as varied as humans can be. For every wild Bohemian there is a Larkin, or a

Trollope, who famously began writing at 5.30 each morning and finished at breakfast-time, after which he went off to his regular work as a clerk, and later as an editor. Few of us perhaps can maintain such self-discipline; however a degree of it is an essential part of a writer's personal equipment, if they are to achieve any reasonable sort of output.

Those who can maintain a steady job and still make time to write may seem to have the best of both worlds – reliable income and a creative outlet. But there is usually a sacrifice to be made, since writing is a time-consuming business and one must eat and sleep sometime. Often you will have to forgo a social life and accept the consequence: loneliness goes with the territory. Indeed writing is perhaps the loneliest of professions, now that there are no lighthousekeepers left. There is no avoiding it: in order to have time to write properly, you are going to have to give up something.

It also helps enormously if you are prepared to accept the insecurity of the writing profession, even if few people would wish to embrace it with open arms. The roller-coaster, feast-or-famine nature of the average writer's life would probably become unbearable to many people. I used to be asked, at times, what I earned for particular pieces of work and when, unwisely, I once mentioned having received a cheque for more than £2,000 the news was greeted with cries of incredulity and envy. The trick on these occasions is to ask the other people how long they would be prepared to work for the same sum. This obliges them to do some mental arithmetic before arriving at a figure of, say, two months. My reply (and it was only too true) was that the aforementioned sum had to last me for about six months, forcing me to plunge once again into overdraft and fend off prying letters from the bank.

The feast-or-famine existence is, of course, the bugbear of all self-employed people, from plumbers to actors (though I've never met a plumber worse off than the actors I know). Spreading an irregular income evenly is a technique not everyone can master, yet writers must do so for they are more vulnerable than most. Books and plays take months and years to complete, and living on an advance or a down payment can be at best difficult, at worst soul-destroying. The moral of all this is embrace the roller-coaster life, if you are temperamentally suited to do so – and have an understanding partner. But whether you are suited to this lifestyle or not, you will probably have to find an additional, regular source of income. I repeat that you must be honest with yourself: are you really cut out for this kind of existence? Answering truthfully is the first step to forging a practical writing life for yourself. If you are not prepared to be hard-up some of the time – perhaps desperately so – then you must face the fact that you can only give a part of yourself to writing. Total commitment to the craft requires sacrifice – and ideally, a private income.

Having accepted that you need money to pursue a writing career, at least in its early stages (and perhaps for longer than many like to think), what sort of work should you do? Or perhaps the question should be rephrased: What sort of work can you do?

I have met writers at all stages of their careers (including, alas, many who weren't writers at all but soldiered on just the same), who have solved the problem of bringing in a basic income by various means. They range from those with full-time jobs who manage against the odds to make regular time to write, to those who have taken the plunge and given up regular employment to write full-time. Some people of course, may have little choice in the matter. Particularly over the last twenty years, redundancy has been seen by many as the opportunity they needed to get down to writing at last, cushioned by a lump sum payment which may support them for a year or two. Unemployment is a major factor in producing new writers; indeed State benefits of one sort or another have constituted a major source of arts funding in this country for years.

If you are unemployed and have the idea of trying to become a writer (and why shouldn't you?), I would offer one or two caveats. Firstly, do not pin your hopes on success, for even if you find you are able to write something to a reasonable standard, the rewards are likely to be at best small and a long way off, at worst non-existent. The second point to remember is that unemployment will not last indefinitely; if you are drawing unemployment benefit you are expected to be actively seeking work which means applying for jobs, attending interviews, job clubs and the like, and unless you can show very good reason why you have been unable to find work, you may lose your benefit.

We touch now on the role of the Supportive Partner, which is crucial to the writer's well-being. It is a complex area, requiring sensitive negotiation, or perhaps naked self-interest. There are almost as many examples of partners who have not only assisted writers' careers, but often moulded and even created them, as there are writers. Two who come readily to my mind are the respective wives of Jeffrey Archer and the 'marquis' de Sade. Lord Archer has freely admitted that after he was declared bankrupt and had decided to try and forge a new career as a novelist, he lived off his wife for two years. The 'marquis' de Sade, on the other hand, seldom gave anyone else credit for anything, but in fact it was his long-suffering wife, Renée-Pélagie de Montreuil, who supported him during his long years in prison, providing him with everything from writing materials, food hampers and linen, to ointment for his haemorrhoids. Without a supportive partner, it seems evident that neither man would have become a writer. Yet here lies another danger: for every unselfish, encouraging spouse in literary history, there is also a Svengali, from whom some writers are not strong-willed enough to free themselves. The French novelist Sidonie Gabrielle Colette was initially nurtured and published by her first husband, but his influence was excessive, and happily, after she broke away from his tight control and divorced him, she went on to forge her own career and produced better work as a result. The Supportive Partner will reappear throughout this book, touching as he or she does on almost every facet of the writer's life. If we may get down to brass tacks, the first step towards financial viability is to work out the minimum you need to live on. If you have a wife, husband, or partner, this must of course be a joint decision. For the time being let us assume that you the writer, with your spouse or partner, have looked at your expenses and arrived at an agreed minimum wage for your household. This must be a realistic figure, subject to review at agreed intervals if arguments are to be avoided later (they will, alas, crop up anyway). How then is that income to be generated, leaving sufficient time to write?

Before looking at the options, it must be said that all of this presupposes that you are prepared to set aside regular writing time: this is imperative. Even two hours a day is enough to produce a reasonable body of work if you use the time well. If you are a fairly new writer, you may not yet have discovered your optimum writing time. For many, myself included, mornings are best; others prefer the night. The luckiest are those who can write at any time, though it does seem to me, after many years of writing, that time of day is less important than it used to be. (Samuel Johnson wags the finger at us all once again: 'A man may write at any time if he will set himself doggedly to it.') Generally I work office hours, starting at 9 a.m. and doing more or less a full day, although creative energy seems to flag by mid-afternoon. Some writers use the less creative hours to do their administration, shopping, walking the dog, or whatever – routines vary. Above all I admire those who, against considerable odds, make time to write when their lives are already hectic. I believe Fay Weldon, with a house full of young children, used to write in the early mornings before they woke up. Some decades earlier, Rumer Godden was doing the same, rising at 4 a.m. and writing for three hours before her two children awoke. One writer I know, a busy head teacher with two children, manages somehow to find time to write very funny plays and pantomimes. Determination is the watchword here.

The options, then, are on the face of it deceptively simple:

(a) full-time employment with time allotted for writing
(b) part-time employment with greater amount of time allotted for writing
(c) full-time writing supported by other means

Full-time Employment with Time Allotted for Writing

This is the most difficult way to develop a serious writing career, though as we have seen, some people have managed it. Usually a full-time job takes not only most of your time but most of your energy too, particularly nowadays. Most people I know seem to be working harder, and for longer hours, than they have done for decades. Nevertheless, if you are unable or unwilling, for whatever reason, to give up the day job yet are still determined to write, you must find a way to do both. If you have a family, even the most heartless mother or father will find their writing time further diminished. Whatever your circumstances, however, if you take a hard look at your situation and are prepared to give something up, golf, embroidery, going to the pub or cinema, even sex, you can probably create a regular slot in which to write. My advice therefore, runs as follows:

1 Don't try and write when you're tired out, for example, straight after coming home from work. Writing takes more energy than most people think.
2 Create a proper writing space where you keep your materials, and, most importantly, where you won't be disturbed.
3 Make this a regular appointment, and stay with it even if you end up sitting there sharpening pencils for two hours. Gradually this writing time will become a part of your day.
4 Draw up some sort of schedule; for example, if you're writing a novel, try to write several pages at each sitting. Even if you only write two pages a day, you can in theory write a 70,000-word book in around six months.
5 Be selfish and make it clear to family and friends that you are not available at this time, for anything other than a real emergency.
6 Finally, be deaf to all criticism from both non-writers and other writers.

Part-time Employment with More Time Allotted for Writing

While this is in theory the ideal way in which to begin developing a writing career, and has worked for a lot of people, like any other method it has its drawbacks. A glance at my local newspaper reveals a rather depressing selection of part-time jobs available, almost all of them poorly paid. If you have a particular skill – plumbing for some reason, comes to mind once again – and can schedule your work leaving regular hours free to write, you are better placed than most. However, this requires a hardheaded determination not to take on jobs which will upset your routine, and you may well lose business as a result. Those with office skills, or secretarial experience have an advantage, for part-time vacancies do occur in this field and it may be worth your while taking a course and acquiring a new skill, or brushing up an old one (ask at the Jobcentre or a local training agency). Those who have no particular skills or qualifications must be prepared to do almost anything, from office cleaning to working as a night security guard. George Orwell believed that the writer should work at a manual job like bricklaying, as it is not intellectually demanding, leaving your mind free to invent. Today's writers would seem to be of similar mind on the subject of alternative employment; in a 1998 survey A.S. Byatt advocated gardening, though some might balk at Lucy Ellman's suggestion of prostitution. There are part-time vacancies for cooks, handymen, careworkers, van-drivers; you have to know your capabilities, do some research and try to be flexible. Speaking personally, one category I would wish to avoid at all costs is that of telesales (too awful to elaborate upon).

A part-time job not only brings in a modest income, it helps keep your feet on the ground and acts as an antidote to one of the writer's occupational hazards, getting out of touch. It can also provide you with a store of experiences which may or may not be useful later on in your writing. But finding part-time work can be difficult. Employers will often fight shy of taking on someone who says they're a writer, for reasons too tiresome to go into, so it is probably best not to mention it. And despite the fact that jobs like garage cashiers, bar staff and the rest would appear to require little in the way of skills and/or experience, competition may be more fierce than you expect, and employers irritatingly choosy. Once you have made the decision to work part-time, you can make a thorough search in the local press and Jobcentres to see what is available in your area, as well as approaching some firms or organizations directly to see if they have any vacancies (though promises to keep your details on file seldom, in my experience, come to anything).

All this, of course, is probably nothing more than common sense. Very few writers start out as writers but work at other things when they first leave school or higher education, and hence most will be able to decide for themselves what they are able to do in the way of part-time work. My advice to the part-time writer would be broadly the same as that given to the full-time worker, with two important exceptions. Firstly, writers with more time to write, are naturally able to increase their output considerably. Indeed it is possible, writing every morning or evening, or at least for a regular number of hours each day, to think more like a professional and treat your writing as a part-time business, which in effect it is, even if you are not yet selling any work. Secondly, writers with part-time jobs have to learn to live on a small amount of money. This may seem glaringly obvious, but those who have previously enjoyed the salary generated by a full-time job often find it difficult to adjust to life on a much lower income. Economy is the watchword here, and writers the world over are experts on the subject. They buy their clothes at Oxfam, they seldom go out, they never buy a drink, they never redecorate the house, they wear the same old sweater for years – the clichés are not without foundation. Even successful writers often exhibit frugal habits which are hard to shake off after years of penury. It is said in Hollywood that writers are the ones who turn up at the Oscars ceremony in rented tuxedos, though this may have little to do with meanness and more to do with the fact that, apart from earning less than almost everyone else in the room, a lot of writers simply hate wearing suits.

Once again, you have to take a hard look at all expenses, and decide what you can live without. To some this may mean simply forgoing the holiday in Spain or the new kitchen (particularly if there is a Supportive Partner bringing in a second income), but for many it is likely to call for more drastic cutbacks: the car, new clothes, bikes for the children, perhaps even moving into a cheaper home. There are few easy options.

Full-time Writing Supported by Other Means

This mode of existence can be blissful, initially anyway – but it can also be sheer hell. While those who can afford, by some fortunate means, to devote themselves to writing full-time may be the object of envy on the part of other writers (and especially of would-be writers), the pitfalls awaiting them can be among the most dangerous of all. If you choose to strike out into chill, choppy waters and become fully self-employed, I strongly recommend some research and planning. Even a cursory glance along the shelves in your local library will reveal that there are various books on the subject.

Being self-employed is not easy. For one thing, many writers find, to their surprise, that they turn out to be very bad employers. They never allow themselves a day off, even when sick, or a proper lunch-break, or holiday pay, or any other perks. In short, they never let themselves forget for one moment that they are working writers: ('a writer', as the saying goes, 'is always in his working clothes'). They become over-anxious to produce work – and even more anxious to sell it – in order to feel like 'proper writers'. In fact, writing doesn't usually happen like that – or at least, not for very many. Some, it is true, respond well to pressure, and even prefer it, like those journalists who, the cliché goes, can't write without a deadline looming over them; for others, it can be a nightmare.

Those who are fortunate enough to have reached the position of being able to write full-time soon find they have a whole new life style to contend with. Firstly, there is the obvious need for self-discipline with nobody to tell them to get to work on time; nobody to stop them staring out of the window, going for long walks or making endless cups of coffee, etc. There is no easy remedy for this, but various techniques do exist to help you get started each morning (what J.B. Priestley referred to as eloquently as 'lifting the elephant off the typewriter'). Having already begun a piece of work before you start as a full-timer helps a great deal: you have something to get on with. If you are in the position of having given up other employment because you are now too busy writing, then you are most fortunate of all, so long as you bear in mind that this situation may not last.

Other problems also begin to surface. One that I had not antici-
pated when I began to write full-time, was that of getting some
people to recognize the fact that I was not merely indulging a
hobby, but was at my desk to work. Knowing that I no longer went
out to a place of work, they thought it perfectly acceptable to ring
me up for a mid-morning chat, or worse still, to drop by and see
how I was getting on ('are you busy, or are you just writing?') Most
irritating of all was to be caught on my daily walk – which I take
partly to get away from the desk and stretch my legs, but sometimes
to think through ideas – by acquaintances who smiled knowingly
before dropping the predictable remark about it being a nice life for
some. It took me years to realize that it is about as easy to try and
explain a writer's life style to non-writers as it might be for an
airline pilot to explain his to a passing seagull.

Most of what I have to say about operating on a day-to-day basis
as a full-time writer will be covered in the next chapter, but there
are two points worth making now. The first is that confidence is
often a fragile thing, and lack of success over a long period embit-
ters many writers. It is better, perhaps, to set yourself a fixed term
in which to try and make tangible progress as a writer, and then be
prepared to do something else if it doesn't work out, at least for a
while; you can return to writing later (although some disagree with
me about this, insisting that you must write every day). The second
point is that self-deception is the most dangerous kind of deception;
the fact that you have been able to arrange your affairs so that you
can write full-time doesn't make you a professional writer. I learned
this many years ago when I was just beginning to write, and a man
I knew from a writers' group phoned to say triumphantly: 'I am
now a writer!' He had taken advantage of a redundancy package
and had given himself a year in which to write. Of course, he had
no commissions, no publisher and, it has to be said, only a modest
talent. As far as I know he sank without trace and is now no doubt
doing some other sort of work.

The paradox is that professional writers themselves sometimes
don't feel like professional writers; in fact the very definition is
open to a number of interpretations. Those who earn a regular
living would no doubt qualify, but would those who are currently

earning nothing from their writing? Being a professional writer, or composer, painter, musician, etc. is something most practitioners work towards, ideally reaching the point where they are so busy with (paid) writing work that there is no room for any other.

It is an intriguing fact of Western society that a surprisingly large number of people yearn to be able to say, 'I am a writer'. I have a lot of sympathy for them, having taught writing workshops and witnessed the participants' often heroic struggles to produce viable pieces of work. But there is a world of difference between wanting to 'be a writer' and wanting to write. Most writers are driven: they must write whatever the circumstances. Yet there is a kind of awe of the profession, even of the very word 'writer', that may evoke pity in the most cynical and hard-boiled 'real writers', including those who sneer at writing courses and blame them for increasing the competition.

If you really want to write and believe that you have enough to live on, from whatever source – Supportive Partner, savings, pension, redundancy pay, inheritance, private income. – I am pleased for you, but I feel compelled to issue further snippets of advice, or, more accurately, warnings: don't fool yourself into thinking that you are a professional writer when you have not yet sold any work; don't feel depressed because you have been sitting at the desk all day and have written nothing – we all have days like that; don't write what you feel you ought to write now that you are a full-timer (like a 250,000-word novel); write what you want to write, however you organize your time and money.

2
Environment

We know virtually nothing about Shakespeare's working methods, except that he wrote, on average, about two plays a year. This, combined with the busy life of an actor, family man and, eventually, shareholder in the Globe Theatre, suggests a considerable degree of application and self-discipline on his part. Genius may account for a great deal, but it is not everything. Presumably even the Bard required somewhere to sit and write, where he would not be disturbed too frequently.

If you are very lucky you may have a room in your home which you can use solely for writing, and which you will no doubt furnish to suit your own tastes (if it has a pleasant view, the old saw runs, turn your desk away from the window to avoid temptation). Others must make do with a desk or table and a comfortable chair, probably in the otherwise least-used part of the home. Where you write is infinitely less important than what you write, so if the top of the stairs, the attic, or a corner of the bedroom works well enough for you, that is fine.

Writers' environments vary a great deal, but with the exception of those who are collaborating – for example television script-writing teams – the vast majority require solitude. Many need peace and quiet, others prefer background noise, some even have music playing'. Dame Daphne du Maurier wrote in a bare, wooden hut in her garden, in which there were only a desk, chair and typewriter (though there was a sea view). Arthur Miller felt he needed to build his own hut in which he then sat down, with the smell of wood-shavings still about him, and wrote the first act of *Death of a Salesman* in a day and a night (other 'garden-shed writers' include Dylan Thomas and George Bernard Shaw). Few would, perhaps, be able (or even inclined) to follow Barbara Cartland's working method of lying on a sofa whilst dictating to a secretary.

If you use the same desk for working and everyday activities like writing letters and paying bills, you will probably find it more difficult to 'clear down' and begin writing in that place, though if you dedicate a certain period of time to writing and nothing else, this difficulty is much diminished. The point is, as I said in the previous chapter, that this is your writing space, and must be used as such. If you have a family or partner, you must persuade them to respect it as a place of work and leave it – and you – alone. ('The only thing you can do for someone who wants to write,' said the American thriller-writer, James M. Cain, 'is to buy him a typewriter.') Most people will understand and get used to the idea; others will take more convincing. What will finally convince almost anyone is your getting something published.

Around you there should be things that comfort you but do not distract you. Many writers' workrooms, which I have seen, are quite spartan and functional, looking, with word processor, phone, fax and perhaps a filing cabinet or two, much like any office does. Some writers are obsessively tidy, others thrive on clutter, though with the arrival of floppy discs we are, at least, no longer obliged to live surrounded by mountains of paper. Bookshelves are common, but not essential, although you do need somewhere to keep reference volumes. Some like to face a bare wall, others have a favourite picture hanging nearby. Roald Dahl – another garden-shed writer – liked to sit in an armchair and write longhand in exercise-books, on a kind of drawing-board on his knees. It matters not at all what your surroundings are like, nor how bizarre your methods. Writers are judged by the works they produce, not by how they produce them.

My own workroom is at the top of the house and has a view of sorts, but my desk faces a plain, white wall with large bulldog clips fixed to it, by which I can attach notes, maps, photographs or anything else relevant to whatever I am working on. My reference shelf is above, where things like dictionaries are within easy reach. The word processor and its printer sit on a lower table at a right angle to the desk. This table has metal legs which I sawed down in order to lower it to the correct height. When you type or use the keyboard, your arms should be parallel to the work-surface, or sloping downwards slightly; if not, you will get writers' cramp which, believe me, is no joke. Repetitive Strain Injury (RSI) is now a regular complaint among those who spend their days at a computer. Headaches and eyestrain are also common. You should have a break from the screen at least every half-hour, taking extra time away at mid-morning, mid-day and mid-afternoon.

I have a few pictures on the walls, but none of them are in my line of vision. The filing cabinet, that I bought second-hand for £30, was an office-grey colour until I sprayed it a warm shade of brown, using car-body paint. The bookshelves are plain pine from a timber-merchant, fixed on adjustable shelving (be assured at this point that DIY skills are not essential to writers). My first desk cost £10 and came from a second-hand office-furniture supplier; later, I treated myself to a more elaborate, eight-drawer affair – but I very much doubt whether I write any better at it.

As should be evident by now, it is not costly to create a place in which to work; someone I know, who writes occasional articles for magazines, used to work at the kitchen table in the evenings, while the children ran about him. Apart from somewhere to sit and keep materials, the writer's needs are surprisingly few. It is important, however, that we spend a little time talking about basic tools and methods.

Tools

Writing Machines

Even if you prefer to work longhand, as some do, you will still need some means of presenting your work in a professional-looking form: nobody reads handwritten submissions. Though it is true, even now, that some writers (particularly those over forty) remain defiantly non-computer-literate, preferring their trusty old typewriters, I find that this attitude is fading fast. In fact, I do not know a single professional writer, in 1999, who does not own a word processor. Some go further and have cheerfully embraced the new technology, updating their hardware and software at every opportunity and using the Internet with confidence.

There is insufficient room in a book of this size for a full discussion of personal computers and word processors. A visit to any large computer store reveals a wide, sometimes baffling array of machines, and an equally wide range of software packages for writing, even for particular kinds of writing (many writers I know use Microsoft Word). I suggest you look closely at what is available, and try the machines out if possible. Staff are generally helpful and will usually demonstrate their wares in some depth (if they won't, I'd go somewhere else). For most writers cost will be a governing factor, but a screen that is easy on the eye is essential, bearing in mind the number of hours you are likely to spend in front of it.

Whether you choose to own a personal computer that will run a range of programs including a word-processing package, or to have a dedicated word processor, you will need to take time to become familiar with the machine. The manuals or user's guides provided are often poorly written, so talking to someone who owns a similar model (if possible) is the best course of action.

Personal computers can cost surprisingly little nowadays, but be wary. Ask detailed questions about the word-processing package that comes with a particular machine, and find out whether it will run alternative software or not. A wide range of fancy-looking fonts is less important than a large memory, for example, or a fast, accurate printer. You also need to be able to move text around comfortably and number pages automatically. To obtain a good-quality machine which can be upgraded and will run a range of software, you may need to spend around £1,000 or more. Your local library will, no doubt, have a range of books about computers, but be warned: these are almost certainly out of date. Developments happen very quickly in this field and things become obsolete, so it is far better to get hold of some magazines (for example *Which Computer?*) and study them. Going on a basic Information Technology (IT) course may also be worthwhile; your local adult education institute or community college probably run classes and if not, they should know who does.

A dedicated word processor – in effect, little more than an electric typewriter with a screen and some memory – is cheaper than a personal computer. Of course, second-hand machines are also available, but I would be wary of them: when things go wrong there is no back-up service to which you may turn. I still use my old Amstrad PCW9512, now coming up to its tenth birthday. Vast quantities of these computers were sold in the 1980s and a surprising number of writers still have them, even though the machine is now virtually obsolete and its distinctive 3-inch floppy discs are no longer manufactured (though it is possible to have the disc drive converted to take standard 3½-inch discs). Over the years I have come to know my machine intimately, have become tolerant of its quirks and habits and think of it not so much as a tool but as an indispensable colleague and ally. It only has the one font, pica, but this has proved to be all I need to produce a typescript of sufficiently good quality. Supplies, including print-ribbons and recycled 3-inch discs (from Italy), are still available at time of writing from Locomotive Software.

Some writers have already dispensed with the time-consuming and costly business of printing out long typescripts and posting them to publishers and editors; they merely send a disc, which can be run on any compatible machine. This is a development that, sooner or later, we cannot afford to ignore.

The Internet

It is becoming increasingly clear that the Internet is going to be part of everybody's future, and in this writers are no exception. For example, writers may advertise their works on the Net and thus gain access to markets world-wide which they never knew existed. Websites are mushrooming daily, and a growing number offer useful information and facilities for writers, including such things as script layouts that can be downloaded, as well as up-to-the-minute databases for areas like publishing. While some of us may cringe at this encroaching phenomenon, in the long run we ignore it at our peril.

For the immediate future, however, it is not essential for a writer to be connected, though many find the use of e-mail convenient and even enjoyable.

The Phone and Fax

The telephone is the bugbear of all writers; we need it, yet at times we loathe it, particularly when it rings just as we are writing the most beautiful sentence or line of dialogue we have invented in months. Consequently an answering machine is fairly indispensable, as you may well want to work for sustained periods without interruption. Many writers hide behind the message on their answering machines, returning calls during their less-creative or administrative periods. Yet sometimes the people we may rely on – agents, producers, editors – require a quick response to some query, and the telephone is their usual means of obtaining it. The phone is fairly essential, particularly for writers who live in the depths of the countryside. And for writers, the reverse of the old saw about bad news travelling fast is often true. Almost all the pieces of good news I have ever received, like a decision to commission a work, have come via the telephone. Those sending out unpleasant things like rejections usually prefer to do so by letter.

I recommend fitting a telephone extension, a simple operation which you can perform yourself. Extension kits (with full instructions) are available from retailers like Dixons or the BT Shop. Since I ran a phone line to my office (total cost, including phone, £22) I have found life a great deal easier. Not only do I no longer have to run downstairs to answer the thing, but when talking about work I have all information readily to hand (I refuse to own a mobile phone).

Many writers nowadays own or rent fax machines. They are not cheap – reasonable quality combined phone-and-fax sets start at around £200 – but if you need to send a lot of material by fax, the machine will eventually pay for itself. You can, of course, go to the local library or post office and even some supermarkets have fax machines. To send a one-page fax from my local post office costs about £2. Bear in mind that the sight, let alone the sound, of incom-

26

ing faxes can be an annoying distraction. Some writers (journalists especially) rely on the fax, others rarely use it. Clearly one must weigh up the cost against the benefits; if you find yourself increasingly having to go out and send faxes from the library or post office, perhaps it is time to invest in your own machine.

Materials

The materials you use for writing will, of course, depend on personal preference. When working longhand, making notes, or roughing out ideas I use wide-ruled, A4 pads of paper – Woolworths is usually an economical option – on which I scribble with complete abandon using a variety of pens. There are generally a dozen assorted ball-points, roller-balls, felt-tips and pencils on the desk at any one time. I like Bic medium pens for fast writing, Berol Fineline for, say, signing letters or correcting typescripts. I also use coloured crayons and highlighter pens to mark manuscripts, research notes and the like. I buy reams of cheap photocopy paper for printing, though for good-quality print-outs it pays to have a supply of heavier-weight paper. If you know someone who works in an office, you might ask them if their employer will sell them a ream at cost price. For rough drafts I use the backs of old scripts.

Stationery prices vary considerably, so rather than merely buying from the nearest high street store you should shop around. Office superstores like Staples are worth visiting, especially for things like small envelopes, which are best bought in bulk packs of fifty or a hundred. To save the expense of having personal stationery printed, you can make up your own letterheads on a word processor. I salvage anything and recycle paper, paper-clips and especially envelopes whenever possible. When a brown A4 or A5 envelope arrives in the post, you can usually unseal it without tearing the flap. The postmark and address can then be covered with a sticky label and the envelope can be reused. Oxfam produce pads of recycled labels bearing the legend 'This Label Saves Trees'; if you prefer not to hammer this message home to the addressee, you can always cut it off.

Photocopying

Sooner or later you will be confronted by one of the writer's heaviest expenses: photocopying. The fortunate will have a friend or relative with access to free (or at least clandestine) photocopying, but bear in mind that repeated requests for six copies of large manuscripts may cool even the best of relationships (and perhaps cause problems with employers). However, if the employers of a friend, relative, or Supportive Partner are sympathetic, it might be possible to do a deal with them to photocopy on their machine at cost price, which means an enormous saving. Paying the full price of anything up to 14p per sheet at a high street copy shop is, in my view, not an option. A 200-page book, for example, is going to cost well over £20 to copy. Public libraries are cheaper, but you are unlikely to be able to copy more than a few pages on their copier before an angry queue builds up. Some community centres offer cheap photocopying facilities, and students normally have access to copying at cost price. (While I must not advocate your infiltrating the local university or college, a little imagination in this area could produce results.) You have to hunt around and badger everyone you can think of; you may be surprised at how many people, once they learn you are a writer, are willing to help.

Some writers have invested in their own photocopiers. Small desk-top machines are not very expensive, but they are often infuriatingly slow. Second-hand machines can sometimes be obtained from office-equipment suppliers and it may be worth phoning a few of them. But unless you plan to do an enormous amount of copying I would not recommend buying a machine. They are often difficult and messy to maintain, and if they break down the cost of getting an engineer in to do repairs can be prohibitive.

Research

Whatever kind of writing you do, whether in the realms of fiction or non-fiction, plays or novels, prose or even poetry, you will probably find that you need to embark on research at some point. For some, this is a pleasure; in fact a common pitfall for many writers is finding themselves seduced into fascinating sidelines by things they discover, thereby losing sight of their original objectives. For others, it is a necessary evil, a diversion from the more important business of actually writing.

Ann Hoffmann's excellent *Research for Writers* will answer almost any question you are likely to have about where to find information.

You need to be aware of what your local libraries have to offer, as their stock may include specialist collections like Local History. Some writers find that membership of a subscription library (like The London Library) is essential, but the fees are not small.

For professional writers, research is a tax-deductible expense, and some are adept at turning weekends by the sea into research trips, claiming for the cost of hotel rooms, boat trips and the like. In recent years, however, the Inland Revenue has begun to look more closely at such items, so before making similar declarations it is wise to ensure that they can be justified.

Research is time-consuming and should not be undertaken lightly. Obviously, if you are writing a realistic novel set during the Napoleonic Wars, you will be expected to know your period and setting thoroughly and will need to steep yourself in it. If you have specialist knowledge, you have a distinct advantage, but do heed a word of caution: certain periods of history have been plundered exhaustively by writers (the English Civil War, the Victorian era, etc., etc.) and publishers are likely to take a great deal of convincing that your book has something new to say. Originality is the watchword; however, if you are passionate about a particular time or place and are burning to write about it, this is often a healthy impulse and it may bear fruit eventually.

You must be realistic about research. If you are a new writer embarking on, say, your first novel, is it worth while spending weeks or months researching the background to a work that is set against the backdrop of the Boer War or the 1926 General Strike? You will need to read quite a lot of books and probably look at photographs, documents, diaries, even archive film if possible, before you can write with real authority about any period. Might it not be better to stay with a subject closer to home? But then, perhaps you have already heard the cliché 'write about what you know', and been bored by it; others have rejected it, and benefited from so doing. I do not advocate merely writing about what you know. In some of my plays I have tackled subjects I knew next to nothing about until I did my research. My feeling is that you should follow your instinct and write about what you care about. If this means that you need to investigate something with which you are unfamiliar, then by all means do research. It may only involve a few trips to the local reference library. If you do not know where to look for the information you want, ask the staff; they are almost always, in my experience, very helpful. If it involves a greater degree of work, and you are prepared to invest the time (and hence the cost), pursue it anyway – the rewards might prove considerable.

Methods

By the time you have been writing for a year or even less, you will probably have found the conditions that suit you best, as well as particular working methods and materials. There are, of course, no rules here, as the examples given earlier suggest; however, as is so often the case, experience is the best teacher, so let me share some of mine with you.

Nowadays I write books more than anything else, and usually work directly on to the word processor. Using double-spacing, I can see an entire page on the screen, which gives me a good idea of what it will look like when printed. In earlier days, however, I often worked longhand, and still do at certain times. Some writers (including distinguished figures like Clive Barker, Barbara Trapido and Alan Sillitoe) extol the virtues of the almost sensual feel of the pen as it moves across the paper, the fluidity of it, the immediacy, the speed and the sheer joy of creating words with your own hand. I admit that this method does work. I once sat down in the proverbial heat of inspiration and wrote the first draft of a thirty-minute radio play in longhand, in one day, pausing only for a quick lunch; however, I do not advocate this as a regular working method. Generally, it is better to work at a steady speed until you find your optimum pace, which, of course, varies from writer to writer. Some set themselves a target of, say, 3,000 words a day (about ten to twelve pages, depending on the typeface you use); others work in intensive bursts of activity. Whether you write longhand or work at the screen, if you find your writing speed increasing as you progress, it is probably a healthy sign, and most writers will tell you, if you find yourself on a roll, stay with it until it either comes to some sort of ending, or you collapse from exhaustion.

Finding the sort of writing that suits you best will be looked at in the next chapter. Let us assume for the moment that you have an idea which you want to pursue. Ideally you should know what sort of length you are working towards, whether it be a 70,000-word book, a thirty-minute comedy script, a full-length play (say, two hours of performance time), a short story, or whatever. You can then try to pace yourself accordingly, setting targets if it helps you. A novel or full-length play, despite all the anecdotes you may hear to the contrary, will probably take months, perhaps years of work; a short story might take you hours, or weeks. For every account of a writer who knocked out a celebrated *opus* in a short time – Oscar Wilde writing *The Importance of Being Earnest* in three weeks is a favourite one – there is a contrary tale of someone who spent years and years on a particular work – James Joyce writing *Ulysses* is an obvious example.

Nowadays I usually plan my works out in advance, mapping out, for example, the number of chapters of a novel, as well as what will happen in each chapter. Drawing up such a scheme provides a useful, reassuring framework, which need not, of course, be adhered to. In certain cases, with regard to a non-fiction book for example, a publisher will expect a complete chapter-by-chapter synopsis from the writer in advance, as well as an estimate of the number of words. If you are a new writer, however, you will probably find this a daunting prospect, and if you are embarking on a work of fiction it might be best if you merely write whatever comes to mind; you can always cut and shape it later.

Getting Started

Whatever you intend to work on, by whatever means, at whatever time of day and in whatever surroundings, there comes a time when you must sit down, try to empty the mind of all its day-to-day clutter and start writing. It matters not a jot now whether or not you have created the ideal conditions in which to work, if you can't get the book, script, or story moving. Some find getting started a tortuous struggle; to others it comes easily. How-to-write books are full of techniques for focusing or concentrating, some of which may work for one person but not for another. The most helpful book on this subject, in my experience, is *Becoming a Writer* by the American tutor Dorothea Brande, first published in 1934.

I tend to agree with Hazlitt, who wrote: 'We never do anything well till we cease to think about the manner of doing it.' Writers develop their own ways of working, often unwittingly. These range from simply waiting for ideas to come (Malcolm Bradbury, for example, likes to sit and think for half an hour each day before commencing writing), to performing exercises in order to free the creative (right-hand) side of the brain, although some professionals will sneer at this. You can attend classes and workshops, often of the weekend variety, with titles like Unlocking the Imagination or Freeing the Creative Spirit. Most writers claim that they simply get an idea, sit down and start working, or, conversely, sit down and work until they get an idea. Many find that they get ideas while doing other activities, sometimes at unlikely times of the day or night (Thackeray apparently leaped out of bed and danced joyfully about the room when he hit upon the title for *Vanity Fair*).

Ibsen kept a small collection of wooden animals on his desk which he used when writing his plays (though exactly how, he did not reveal). Some writers like to have prints or photographs pinned up over the desk as a stimulus; others use videos. Notes are useful to refer to, at least as an antidote to the notorious clean sheet of paper or blank screen that confronts you when you begin a new piece of work. Many start the day by reading over what they wrote the day before, then continuing from there. Hemingway's *A Moveable Feast* contains some useful ideas, in particular his method of writing continuously until he had produced something worth saving, and then putting down his pencil when he knew what was coming next. Some writers even like to finish the day's work in mid-sentence: that way it is easier to resume work tomorrow.

All we are talking about are ways of allowing the subconscious to do its work, for this is where the 'creative' part of writing happens, while the conscious mind, taking care of the 'craft' component, shapes and orders the material. Every artistic endeavour is a combination of creation and technique; it is no use having a beautiful vision if you are unable to capture it on paper, canvas, or in some other form. Technique is learned over a period of time, and like anything else, it improves with practice (if it doesn't, you are probably in the wrong field). Any television script editor will tell you that they receive hundreds of ideas every year for series, serials and single dramas which are never realized because the person with the idea, no matter how promising it may be, is unable to write it in a workable form.

Keeping Going

Starting a piece of work can be relatively easy; seeing it through to the end is usually much harder. Leaving aside the difficulties inherent in the piece itself, there are times when, faced with innumerable hazards, it seems like a daily battle to get anything written at all.

Psychologists talk about displacement behaviour, which means, broadly speaking, doing one thing in order to avoid confronting something else. Writers are especially prone to this syndrome and most have fallen into the trap at one time or another – anything to put off the awful moment of having to start work. The Elizabethans no doubt sharpened their quills, refilled their inkpots and fiddled with their flea-combs for an hour or two before forcing themselves to write a sentence. Later generations of writers have followed suit: sharpening pencils, sorting out their bookshelves, filing their manuscripts. Nowadays there are even more temptations like surfing the Net, checking your e-mail, or copying a disc. Staring out at the scenery no doubt remains as popular now as it once was with Homer or Sophocles.

Aside from the techniques mentioned earlier, like Hemingway's, you must be prepared to try different working methods until you find one that gets you going, for example, starting at a different time of the day; indeed many how-to-write books advise rising early and beginning work at once. There are no easy answers. In the end, if you are a writer, you can and must make yourself write. If you are stuck you might begin by writing a letter to someone you rarely see, like a relative you loathe; even if you never send it, it gets the juices flowing. I sometimes read some non-fiction, like a page or two of a biography to silence the 'fool in the head' (the busy conscious mind), as well as reading over yesterday's work and starting from there.

There are a few solutions I might offer to the perennial problems of distractions and interruptions. As I wrote this a police siren wailed in the distance, taking my mind off the sentence; fortunately I was able to keep it in focus. Unless you can soundproof your workplace, or live in the deepest countryside (and noises exist there too), noise will sometimes be a problem. In a remote cottage in Cornwall, I was regularly woken at an unsociable hour by the braying of a donkey in a nearby field. Some things cannot readily be eliminated. Double-glazing helps, for example, against traffic noise, and you will probably work at the back of your house or flat anyway. Traffic noise, however, becomes a mere background rumble and is not particularly disruptive if you stop listening to it. Noise caused by neighbours can pose a much more serious problem, and tact is required unless you wish to be featured on one of those painful-to-watch television documentaries. Explaining politely to people that you are a writer who is trying to work can sometimes produce a sympathetic response, particularly if you are prepared to be economical with the truth ('I can't say too much, but the publisher/BBC/film company are hounding me to get it finished . . .'). If all else fails, you can always use ear plugs (Boots sell them at a reasonable price).

I have suffered from various kinds of noise, at various addresses. The worst problem was caused by 'difficult' (I use the word carefully) neighbours playing loud music. Attempting to remonstrate with them produced only threats and abuse. In a situation like this, feuding is upsetting and can even stop you writing. The local authority (Environmental Health Department) can and will act if you complain to them, but the process is lengthy and involves things like your monitoring the level of noise and keeping a log of when it takes place. Better, perhaps, to soundproof the wall or ceiling, move to another room if possible, use ear plugs (though they are a constant reminder of the problem and can make you feel resentful), or even move house (which we eventually did). If working at home really is impossible at any time, the local reference library or reading-room can be a welcome refuge. Some writers maintain that a favourite café is a good place in which to work, though presumably it's wise to choose one where you will be left undisturbed with your coffee for long periods. Failing everywhere else, there is always a quiet corner of the pub.

Another serious intrusion I experienced at home was the daily sound of a dog barking nearby. Some years ago there was an item on the news about a man who had been prosecuted for hitting his neighbour over the head with an iron bar. I recall being shocked until I learned that the man had been driven to such desperate measures by the neighbour's dog, which had barked loudly and persistently for months, perhaps years. One or two writers I know incline to the view that dog owners who exhibit this degree of selfishness should perhaps be hit regularly with iron bars, for nothing else seems to persuade them that others have a right to a little peace and quiet.

Interruptions can and must be guarded against. We are all, like Coleridge, victims, at sometime or other, of Persons from Porlock. Working feverishly on 'Kubla Khan' at his cottage in Somerset, Coleridge was interrupted by a visitor, 'a person . . . from Porlock', on business. By the time the man had gone the unfortunate poet had lost his train of thought and never got it back. The work remained forever unfinished.

I return to the point already made about getting people to realize that you must be left alone to write. When I am settling down to work, my method is simple: the answering machine is switched on, the doors are locked and will not be opened. I am at work, and will be available again when I have finished, like anyone else at the end of a working day. Some might call this behaviour selfish; I prefer to call it being professional.

3
What Sort of Writer Are You?

There are many examples of successful writers who began by doing one sort of writing, only to find later that they were better suited to another. Philip Larkin, arguably the finest poet of his generation, started out hoping to succeed as a novelist, but few are aware of his novels today. Some novelists began as journalists, scribbling stories in their spare time. More will be said about diversifying in the next chapter; for the present, a brief survey of the main fields of writing may help you in making your mind up as to what sort of writer you are: poet, playwright, novelist, or whatever. This is not to say that you cannot do more than one kind of writing; indeed, many do, myself included. But if you have a particular talent in one field it would seem a pity not to make the best use of it.

The Novel

If literary fiction is your field, you will, no doubt, be an avid reader of it. Some maintain that this is not essential, but I believe it is useful to have read some of the classics, especially the great novelists, and not only those writing initially in English. Presumably, if you have an urge to write a novel, you will also have an idea of what it will be about, and will, perhaps, have made a few notes, or even a plan.

There are a number of how-to-write books dealing with the novel, but I decline to recommend a particular one, as I have generally found them to be of limited value. The advice given varies, so that while some, for example, advocate meticulous planning of each chapter, others tell you to work steadily through from beginning to end without referring to plans or looking back.

It should do no harm, if you have tried other forms of writing, to attempt to write your novel; indeed, this is the only way to discover whether or not the form suits you. Aside from novellas, which seldom get published unless written by an established writer, the shortest acceptable novel is likely to be around 50,000 words long, an average is around 70,000 and many are much longer. It is easy to calculate that 70,000 words – even if your output amounts to a steady 3,000 words a day, which is hard work – is going to take weeks of solid effort, and probably much longer (many spend several years on one book). You must also engage the reader's attention at every stage with an enticing beginning, a middle that wants them to keep on reading and a satisfying ending (though this last is not always essential). If you find that you can sustain your pace without flagging after a couple of weeks (though any writer can wane on occasion), then perhaps the novel form suits you. I recommend reading through the previous chapter each time you settle down to write, then continuing at once. Once a week or so, you might also read through the whole book from the start, though some prefer not to do this. When you reach the end, apart from celebrating, or merely collapsing, it is wise to put the thing aside for a while, even for weeks, and do something else before looking at it again (Joe Orton's system of putting his manuscripts in a drawer to 'mature' for three months before rewriting, works for many).

At time of writing, the market for novels is still fairly healthy, as is evident from the frightening 9,000 fiction titles published, on average every year (since 1994). Pronouncements by various critics that 'the English novel is dead' would seem to be greatly exaggerated. Thankfully, people still want to read such books, so why should you not write yours? And if you are a fairly new writer, even if you abandon your novel it does not mean that you cannot write another. I wrote plays for almost twenty years before writing my first novel; I now find the form deeply satisfying. However, taking on such a long piece of work can be a daunting task for a first-timer, and some lose heart. Having a strong story to tell, perhaps drawn from a family source, is a good starting point. Try to pace yourself and stay with it, and the rewards could one day be considerable. If, on the other hand, you have tried several times to write a novel, and have given up, maybe you should cut your losses and try another field.

Theatre

It is difficult to write, in 1999, about the current state of the theatre in the UK, and about theatre writing in particular, without quickly becoming depressed. *The Stage & Television Today* of 18 February 1999 reports that 'as few as three regional producing theatres in England are likely to end the financial year in the black without the aid of stabilization funding'. Every week another theatre seems to be facing serious financial shortfall, even closure, while touring companies lose their subsidies and go under at an alarming rate. The non-subsidized theatres, i.e. those in the West End of London, do mainly musicals, revivals of popular comedies and classics, and are not a market for the unestablished writer. Those theatres which still produce new plays do fewer of them, or co-produce with other theatres (in other words, only one writer gets employed where once there were two). And when they do commission a play by a living playwright, instead of merely performing the work of dead ones, they are likely to play safe and work with a writer who is well established. The number of theatres that do new writing has shrunk to a stalwart few which take pride in the fact. Most are in London – the Royal Court Theatre and the Bush Theatre are perhaps the best known – but not all, the West Yorkshire Playhouse in Leeds being a well-respected exception.

Other theatres and theatre companies that are obliged by funding criteria to do new plays, get round the 'problem' by calling a translation of a successful foreign play, or a version of a classic, a 'new' play. Another favourite is the 'company-devised work': rather than hire a writer, the actors and director make a play up themselves in the rehearsal room. Not surprisingly, the standard of many such pieces leaves a lot to be desired.

New writing, it is constantly said, loses money (though there are arguments to the contrary), and not surprisingly, this area is the first to suffer when funding cuts are called for, which they are every year. The Royal Shakespeare Company got rid of its Literary Manager a few years ago and disbanded his department, giving a clear signal that it would be futile for anyone to send them a new play in the foreseeable future. In 1995 the Bristol Old Vic Theatre announced (at least they were honest) that they would be introducing a reading fee of £10 for unsolicited scripts, which would stand little chance of production in any case. A general mood of gloom pervades any gathering of playwrights these days, with everyone struggling not to face the common view that the audience for theatre is disappearing, and that the future for theatre writing is more or less doomed. This is even more dangerous than it sounds, for new writing is in fact the life-blood of theatre. All plays were once new. Without new writing the theatre is merely a museum, a platform for recycled plays and new interpretations of the classics. Theatre is a main plank of our culture and of our heritage, and some believe it is in more danger now than it has ever been.

In fact, the position is not (not yet, anyway) quite as desperate as that, but let me state personally that while writing for live performance is my own abiding passion, it is also the area in which I have had most disappointments, bad experiences, shabby treatment and probably earned the least income. Theatre is the sexiest yet most demanding medium of all, and you engage with it at your own risk.

There are no short cuts to getting a play professionally produced – though cynics maintain that it helps if you are under thirty, have been treated for drug abuse, or have an Irish name – and if it is a steady, reasonable income you seek, forget about writing for the theatre *now* and move to the next subheading. The main requirement is that you are passionate about live performance, in which case you already go to the theatre and know something about how it works. If not, you must start learning, seeing and reading plays, and even hanging around rehearsal rooms (*not* stage doors) if possible. It may also be worth reading a book such as *Writing a Play* by the respected playwright and director, Steve Gooch. (Mr Gooch, when asked by his students for advice about getting their plays produced used to recommend they hang around in bars – provided they were the right bars.)

In the theatre, in some ways, little has changed in 200 years. When David Garrick sold his share in the Drury Lane Theatre to Richard Sheridan in 1776, unread plays accumulated in piles all over the office. Playwrights complained of receiving neither acknowledgement nor return of their manuscripts. The difference then, was that angry scribes began showing up at the theatre demanding to see the director in person. Today, nobody would even attempt such a strategy, attractive though it sounds. Be prepared, if you send off a play, to receive no reply for up to six months or more, and sometimes, to receive none at all.

Those who write successfully for the theatre usually begin modestly, perhaps taking advantage of the occasional new writing festival at their local theatre and getting a rehearsed reading of a play staged (which means the actors were paid, but the writer got nothing), or writing for amateurs, or putting a small production together themselves (perhaps on the London fringe, and almost certainly for no money). They persist in writing plays and sending them out to theatres and companies, spending huge sums in postage costs and refusing to be discouraged by constant rejection, until somebody, somewhere begins to notice them. One playwright described to me his own tactic of wearing down a director or literary manager with repeated letters and submissions, until the person concerned becomes so exhausted by this bombardment that they feel the only way to get this persistent writer off their back is to give him a commission. I don't pretend that this will work in every case, but there is a great deal to be said for sticking to your guns.

If you are the sort of writer who hates the loneliness of the profession and enjoys working with others, theatre writing may suit you, for theatre is a collaborative art. The difference between this and other sorts of writing is that with a play, the finished script is only a beginning. The writer is then involved in a production process with other creative talents like the director, designer and actors. It is an exciting business, and can be immensely rewarding. It can also, at times, be sheer hell: experiences vary widely.

Successful playwrights often have a strong visual sense, a good ear for dialogue and an instinct for what will work on the stage. Their plays sometimes look quite insignificant on the page until you try them out in performance, whereupon the magic begins to unfold before you. A single gesture or expression in the theatre can say more than a whole speech, and many writers like the sparseness of it, the dynamism, the opportunity to present action and great passion – not to mention the incomparable buzz of seeing your work performed before a live audience who laugh, cry, boo, call out and, if all goes well, even applaud.

If all of this excites you, by all means write plays and send them to theatres, but you would be well advised to contact them first and ask whether they will look at a new play from an unknown playwright. Those who will are becoming an increasingly rare and precious group.

If you have an ear for dialogue, but feel your talents lie in the writing of scripts for a wider audience than that of the theatre, perhaps one of the broadcast media might suit you better.

Television

At a writers' conference I attended a year or two ago, a writer on a well-known soap answered the perennial question of how one breaks into television with a single word: hustle. This is the most competitive medium, partly because it is often the best paid (a writer who works regularly in television can earn a six-figure income), but also because all those who watch television drama think they know how to write it. Scripts wing their way across the country to the BBC and the commercial television companies every week in their hundreds, swelling the coffers of the Royal Mail and generally producing nothing for the writer but disappointment. Needless to say, television is as difficult to write for as any other medium, and more so than most. Gaining a foothold in the industry requires not only essential qualities like talent and persistence, but also the development of a strategy to assail its well-fortified walls, and the tenacity of a medieval foot-soldier.

With television, I believe it is a good idea to consult a few how-to-write books, because there are certain things the newcomer really has to know, like how to lay out a script properly. Nobody in television has time for amateurs or beginners, and a badly presented script will probably be returned unread or conveniently 'lost'. The nature of the business changes rapidly, being driven largely by the ratings war and by commercial considerations in general, so ask at a good book store for the most up-to-date books on writing for television (you may like to start with *How to Write for Television* by William Smethurst). If you write to BBC Television and ask politely they will also send you some writers' guidelines on script layout. Then, when you have written what you are sure is a decent script, you can begin to hustle.

Since the BBC abolished its television script unit (the commercial television companies never really had such units) it no longer has a central office for receiving and assessing scripts, or, more importantly, for discovering and encouraging new writers for the medium; hence, the aspiring television writer must develop a thick skin, for here, perhaps more than anywhere else, rejection is the norm.

However, you might be surprised at how easy it is to get a comedy script looked at; television is always hungry for popular ideas, and a promising concept for a series or even a sitcom might be received with cautious approval. As a newcomer in this area you will need to write a pilot script on spec (i.e. unpaid) and provide outlines for (usually) five further episodes to show the powers that be that you have thought hard about your idea and worked at it. Richard Curtis, perhaps the most successful TV comedy writer of the 1990s, says comedy writers should always write for their own circle: if it doesn't make you and your friends laugh, it is unlikely to make anyone else laugh. BBC Light Entertainment (at the same address as BBC Television Centre) will look at ideas, but the number of submissions they receive is quite frightening. Yours must, of course, be funny, it must be original, it must tell a story people would want to watch on the screen, and it must be technically achievable, ideally as cheaply as possible.

With regard to serious drama, it is a different tale. The days of the single play are over, and it is little use sending in a one-hour television script, for nobody is going to produce it. If it is very good, it might, however, show that you can write for the medium, and if it lands on the right desk . . . such things have happened. But it is pointless sending in an idea (let alone a script) for a four-part adaptation of Dickens, or a three-part thriller. Such programmes are hugely expensive to make and nobody is going to risk that sort of money by commissioning a writer who has no track record in television.

The soaps, which employ teams of writers up to sixteen strong, do occasionally take on new people, but the waiting list is probably vast, and in such an endeavour talent and persistence are simply not enough: you need luck (like being in the right place at the right time). You could write to the producers of your favourite soap and ask to write for them, but they receive many such letters. You could write a script for an episode of your own devising to show how well you know the background, the characters and the soap's style, but it may not even be read for contractual reasons. Most television companies will not read scripts unless they are submitted by an agent. If you do receive a response that is the tiniest bit encouraging – anything apart from an outright 'No' – you would be wise to follow it up at once. Send in further scripts, badger the producers, visit the studios if possible, seek out someone involved in the series – hustle, hustle and hustle again. If not, your name will be forgotten very quickly. Only the most determined souls (and the very lucky) get the chance to write for television. But remember that the output from five terrestrial channels, let alone cable, satellite and the rest, is vast, and television does need a ready supply of ideas, and people to write them. If you want to badly enough, and have a talent for TV writing, persistence here, as elsewhere should, in theory at least, bear fruit eventually.

Radio

Radio is the medium through which the work of many well-known dramatists was first heard, from Tom Stoppard and Joe Orton to Roy Clarke, author of *Last of the Summer Wine*. An extract from

Samuel Beckett's *Waiting for Godot* was broadcast on French radio in 1952, a year before the famous stage premiere, and it is often forgotten that such 1950s television classics as *Life with the Lyons* and *The Glums* started life initially on radio, as did *Hancock's Half Hour*. Radio is very satisfying to write for and also pays reasonably well, with the current rate for established writers at just over £60 per minute, which means roughly £3,600 for a sixty-minute play. BBC Radio drama has allowed many writers to cross that important, morale-boosting Rubicon of having their work professionally produced. Despite various changes and financial cut-backs, at time of writing radio remains the largest single market for plays, producing hundreds of them every year. The first-time writer can still send in a radio play and have it considered. But writing for radio demands the special technique of telling a story without pictures – or rather, creating pictures in the mind of the listener. The writer must think in sound terms first (having a musical ear seems to help); whereas with film or television writing you describe what the camera sees, with radio you describe what the microphone hears.

There are several good books on writing for radio, which the aspiring writer might do well to consult. Donald McWhinnie's classic *The Art of Radio* is now very out of date, but the basic principles laid down still apply. I would recommend William Ash's *The Way to Write Radio Drama* and Colin Haydn Evans' *Writing for Radio*. It is also worth reading published radio plays, like the Methuen collections, available in libraries under the title *Best Radio Plays of 1978* and so on up to 1992, as well as the plays of Tom Stoppard, David Rudkin, Don Haworth and other good writers for the medium. Many distinguished playwrights, including Harold Pinter, John Arden and Margaretta D'Arcy, Howard Barker and Fay Weldon, have written excellent pieces for radio. Most writers speak of the freedom radio offers. Its production costs are also very low compared with television: on radio you can stage the Trojan War for the cost of a few recorded background noises, like some appropriate clanging and shouting.

And yet the axe has fallen on radio during the 1990s as it has elsewhere. Some BBC Radio drama studios, like the excellent Christchurch studios in Bristol, have been closed. The number of weekly slots for plays remains much the same as it has been for decades, but the length of plays now produced has been cut; for example, the ninety-minute Monday Play, a slot much cherished by professional writers, was scrapped. The radio drama script unit, like its television counterpart, was abolished in 1994 and its literary manager Alan Drury, himself a capable writer, was made redundant. Hence writers must now send scripts to individual producers, whose names you can glean from looking carefully through the radio section of *Radio Times* or from a publication like Spotlight Casting Directory & Contacts. There are also a large number of independent radio production companies now, but the majority are very small operations (often run by ex-BBC producers) which only receive a meagre allocation of productions on radio each year. A list of these companies can be obtained from the Writers' Guild of Great Britain.

I strongly recommend regular listening to radio plays, for this is the best way to gain an understanding of how radio drama works, and to build up a picture of the sort of material that is produced. The BBC operates a biannual commissioning policy in which plays are bought in for the next half-year in a batch. The lengths to write for are thirty minutes (usually series and serials, especially comedy), forty-five minutes (the weekday afternoon play) and sixty minutes (the Friday play). Adaptations are always needed but will normally only be commissioned from writers with a track record. The best way to break in is to send a well-written and well-presented script to a producer whose work you like (find out first whether they are based in London or in one of the regional studios). Radio is a particularly good market for comedy, and successful radio series continue to transfer to television. As with television, guidelines for writers are available from BBC Light Entertainment.

If you have not considered writing for radio before, it is well worth doing so – while you still can. What the long-term future of radio drama will be, nobody knows (or if they do, they are remaining tight-lipped about it). In many parts of the world it has disappeared, to be replaced by music programmes, news bulletins and phone-ins. However, the radio networks of many European countries still have a reasonably healthy drama component, and the

BBC, with its unique drama output, is the envy of the world in this respect. Radio is a rewarding field in which to work, and one where the individual writer is still valued and involved; those who work in radio usually try their best to realize the writer's original vision in production. Long may they continue.

Film

A trip to the main library in your region, as well as to the larger bookshops, will usually reveal a number of paperback books with titles like *How to Break into Hollywood* or *How to Make a Million from your Screenplay*. Often they are written by Americans and were first published in the US. A look through the back pages of the arts section of most broadsheets will reveal another curious phenomenon: the abundance of blockbusting courses entitled How to Write a Hit Movie (or words to similar effect), often to be held in hotels in central London and costing several hundred pounds for the weekend (but they will, the advertisement proclaims, tell you 'everything you need to know'). The course is usually run by an 'award-winning' screen-writer, though surprisingly the name is not one you recall hearing before. In fact many (not all, admittedly) of the men – they are always men – who run such courses have made a steady living by writing screenplays for films that have never been made. The system being what it is, a writer who is hired to write a film script gets to keep the fee, or a portion of it, even though the film never goes into production. Most screenplays that are written never reach the screen; hence, the newcomer attempting to enter the world of writing for film must develop the toughest skin of all. While the fees can be the highest a writer will ever earn – sometimes for top screen-writers, running into millions for one script – the chances of your screenplay transferring to celluloid, or even of being read are very small indeed.

If you are passionate about getting into film, you can get hold of published film scripts and study their style and technique. You will already be a movie buff, and can, no doubt, talk knowledgeably about the work of Truffaut, Wim Wenders or Oliver Stone. You were probably hooked at the age of six when your parents took you to *The Wizard of Oz, Pinocchio* or *E.T.* You have seen every movie Hitchcock/John Ford/Kubrick (alter as appropriate) made, and can even name the screen-writers. If you are lucky enough to get a place at film school you can, perhaps, enrol on a screen-writing course; there may even be one run by your local arts centre. The basic structure of film can, many believe, be taught, as can the basics of script-writing (the Americans had writing courses forty or fifty years before they appeared in the UK). More about courses will be said later but for now, let us assume that you have a story that you feel would make a great film. How should you proceed?

The first fact to recognize is that most feature films nowadays are based on books that are already published (and are probably best-sellers), or on well-known events or people, or are sequels to other, already successful films. The film company plans a movie behind closed doors – whether the idea was initiated by a producer, someone on the board or someone else's therapist – and they then commission a writer, or writers. The writer will be someone known to them (for a chilling satire based on some uncomfortable truths about how the Hollywood system operates, see Robert Altman's film *The Player*). Established writers can and do pitch original story ideas to film producers, but few are commissioned, and despite the usual tales to the contrary (for example, how Ronald Neame and David Lean wrote the script of *Great Expectations* in two weeks in a hotel room in Cornwall), writing a screenplay is very hard work. According to its author Richard Curtis, the script of *Four Weddings and a Funeral* underwent at least seventeen rewrites. The phrase 'development hell' has been coined in recent years: few writers emerge from such a place unscathed.

If you are undeterred by all this and have written what you believe is a good film script (and do consult books on how to lay it out, what terminology to use and so on), then the most sensible thing would be to contact a literary agent who handles film (look carefully through *The Writer's Handbook*). Sending it to a film company directly is likely to be a waste of time and postage; many companies listed in handbooks say 'no scripts', 'no unsolicited material', or even 'all work is commissioned from within the company'. A few, however, say they are interested in hearing from new writers, but prefer to receive a c.v. and a synopsis of an idea rather than a script.

If approaching an agent, write or phone first, tell them (briefly) about your script and ask them if they would like to look at it. If they will, send it (with return postage enclosed, naturally), but do not hold your breath. As should be painfully clear by now, the chances of it being made into a film are slim indeed. But in this field as with everything else, there are exceptions, and there are stories, like movies, with happy endings. If the idea of collaboration appeals, you might like to team up with someone who shares your tastes and aspirations and write a script together. The burden is lighter when shared, and each of you will have a shoulder to cry on if rejection follows.

The Screenwriter's Store sells US format paper (American film companies will not even read a script unless it is on their size of paper and bound in their preferred way), as well as books and magazines for writers and screen-writing software.

Short Stories

When I taught classes in creative writing (that irritating, inadequate term), the most common thing beginners would say at the first session was that they'd had an idea they might like to write short stories, perhaps for magazines. The thought of attempting a novel or a play was too daunting for most. Short stories, being short, ought to be easier and quicker to write. Then they could be sent to a magazine and, with a little luck, published.

In fact, not only can short stories be fiendishly difficult to write, but there is very little market for them. A few periodicals do publish them, including some poetry magazines, but they generally require work of a very high literary standard. Collections of short stories are normally published only when they are the work of a well-known author, sometimes as a courtesy or favour by his or her publisher (since they never sell as well as novels). This was not always the case in decades past, and some distinguished writers, it is true, are known for their short stories above all else, like V.S. Pritchett, for example, or Saki. The form has appealed to generations of writers, and still does; it is very satisfying, and yes, it should take less time to write a 1,500- or 3,000-word story than a full-length novel, but some writers spend months on them, writing draft after draft, honing the piece until they feel it cannot be improved. Henry James was famously quoted as saying that he would like to write short fiction, but he didn't have the time.

In very recent times there has been talk of a resurgence in the popularity of the short story, especially with the publication of handy pocket-sized editions for reading on the bus or train. Important contemporary writers such as Martin Amis and Salman Rushdie have produced collections. And since we are said to live in the age of the diminishing attention span, perhaps the short story has a future after all.

There is no harm in writing stories; it is good practice, it helps you find your voice and style and it might even earn you a little money one day, though this is more likely to be from winning a competition than from being published (the one sometimes follows the other). There are dozens of short story competitions every year, sometimes run by writers' circles, with cash prizes for winners and runners-up. Advertisements for them appear in local libraries, arts centres and in writers' magazines. Some writers have indeed begun careers on the strength of winning such competitions, but remember that the number of entries is likely to be large and the standard often high. Not winning a competition is no disgrace, and should be thought of in similar vein to not winning the lottery; the judges are usually writers themselves, with their own tastes and biases (viz. the annual controversy that greets the announcement of the Booker Prize winner).

If it is a serious writing career you seek, short stories alone will not be enough. Agents are not interested in them, and neither is anyone else, apart, perhaps, from your relatives and fellow-students at writing classes. The radio market for stories has almost dried up, though local radio stations sometimes read listeners' stories out on the air and pay a nominal fee of, say, £5 to each writer. A BBC Radio 4 short story commands a fee of about £100, or a little more for the established writer, while magazines, if they publish stories at all, can usually afford only a small payment.

Poetry

If writing short prose is a labour of love, the same is true to an even greater extent with regard to the most refined literary form of all, poetry. The number of poets who earn a living from their work in this country can probably be counted on one's fingers. Practising poets generally supplement their income by other means, and most earn more by giving readings of their work than through publication. There are a few dedicated publishers of poetry, usually tiny and operating on a shoe-string budget, but the readership for poetry is small, and it is often said ruefully by poets that the only people who attend poetry readings are their fellow-poets. Some, it is true, have achieved celebrity status, but this is largely from personal appearances, or in one case by being made Poet Laureate. Some do quite well out of writing popular verse that appeals to, say, children. The serious poet must, however, resign herself or himself to earning a living by other means as, for example, Philip Larkin did (Andrew Motion's biography *Philip Larkin: A Writer's Life*, is worthy of any writer's time). Poetry is, perhaps, something you should write when you feel the urge; indeed, it might well get published, for there are a surprising number of poetry magazines that welcome submissions, of almost any length and on any topic. But when it comes to payment, £5 and a free copy of the magazine are all you are likely to receive.

Submitting Your Work

I feel that a word is called for with regard to submitting work. I credit the readers of this book with the sense not to send out their only copy of a manuscript – things can and do get lost. You should keep copies of everything, including work on floppy disc (even more prone to accidents than printed matter). You should always present your work as professionally as possible, which does not mean using ornate fonts or colour printing, but rather that it should be easy on the eye of a reader who is faced with half a dozen manuscripts to get through before 5 p.m. It means not only (as anyone who attends a writing class knows) double-spacing, with generous margins, on one side only of A4 paper; it means clear page numbering, neat chapter headings, properly laid-out scripts, a stamped addressed envelope for return of your manuscript and a brief, businesslike covering letter. Radio or television scripts should be pinned through the top, left-hand corner using a daisy clip (available from good stationers). Plays can be bound using a slide-binder or, for a professional look, a comb-binder, or spiral ring-binder. Some high street copy shops provide a while-you-wait binding service; it is not very expensive, and the addition of a clear acetate sheet at the front and a stiff card at the back of a script will protect it and add to its shelf-life. A dog-eared manuscript with coffee stains on the front page is not likely to inspire much confidence in an editor or script reader when it arrives on their desk first thing on a Monday morning.

Novels should be printed neatly (double-spacing, of course) and left unbound, packed carefully in a folder or parcel, with a synopsis included. A few minor typescript corrections (made precisely in black ink) are acceptable. Nothing need appear on the front cover except the title and author's name, though it is wise to put your address and telephone number at the bottom in case your covering letter goes astray. I find small, stick-on address labels very useful (a print out of 1,000 of these, self-addressed on a peel-off roll, will be produced by any high street printer at a reasonable cost).

When all is ready, post your manuscript and try to put it from your mind (you will not, of course, succeed in this). Treat yourself to a meal, a drink, or at least a cup of tea (one writer I know always gives herself the rest of the day off after sending out a piece of work), then sit down and start your next piece. You are a working writer now.

4
Diversify or Die

A few years ago, some research into farm diversification for a play I was writing about farming led me to do a little lateral thinking about my own profession. Small farmers in particular, faced with financial problems on a scale I had barely imagined, have long since recognized the need to seek other means of earning an income, from simply starting a farm shop to opening go-kart tracks, or letting their woodland out for paintball games. In this new millennium, when flexibility is the watchword across most fields of industry, writers need to think hard about the sort of work they are doing and ask themselves if there are other areas they might consider. This will, of course, apply less to those who are doing very well in their chosen fields, but increasingly, writers are working across more than one medium or genre. Hardly any, for example, can make a living writing exclusively for radio, and few make a living solely from the theatre. Playwrights often diversify into television or film as soon as the opportunity arises, while novelists may jump at the chance to adapt their work for the screen. There are other reasons for diversifying too: it is sometimes refreshing for, say, a writer of serious novels, to have a stab at non-fiction, or a book for children. Often the writer learns a great deal from doing something else, and their regular work, far from suffering from the change is enriched by the experience.

To some extent writing for different media requires the wearing of different hats, for although the creative process remains broadly the same, you are working within different conventions and restrictions, sometimes employing a specific language (as with a television or radio script). Wearing your romantic novelist's hat, you are probably in a different frame of mind from when you sit down on another occasion to tackle the book you have been longing to write about Victorian chamber-pots, or the biography of Mae West (I think that one's been done). There are difficulties, however, as well as joys, in switching to other areas; as we have seen already, the best way to find out if one suits you more than another is to try it. Let us consider a few options.

Children's Writing

The market here is large and the genre potentially rewarding. There are many publishers of children's books, as a little basic research will verify. They will often expect a book to be illustrated; indeed sometimes the illustrations, particularly with regard to books for younger children, are more important than the text – there may not even *be* any text. Hence, writers who can illustrate are in a potentially strong position. It is worth approaching publishers with an idea, rather than a finished book because the output in children's fiction is so vast that someone else may have already done what you propose.

It is not essential to be a parent in order to write for children. Oddly perhaps, some of the most famous writers of children's books seem to have been very bad parents. Conversely, as always, some of the great children's classics began life by being told as stories before being written down (A.A. Milne's being the most famous example). Some writers like to try out their stories on their own children, but naturally enough there comes a time when this is no longer practical. Others may work within the considerable market for teenage fiction, so offspring of the right age would no doubt be a useful barometer here as elsewhere.

To write well for children you need a feel for the genre – perhaps the ability to become a child yourself while you work, whereupon you write to please yourself (always a good idea in any case). The golden rule, if there are any, is that one must never 'write down' for a young readership, but write as painstakingly and as honestly for them as you would for adults. Children – particularly those under, say, eleven – are a very uncritical audience, eager for information as well as sensation; they are also bored very easily (watch a third-rate children's entertainer at work and note the reactions). Many find writing for children a liberating experience, not to say a lucrative one. If you think you might like to try, get hold of as many children's books as possible and devour them. It is of paramount importance that you are clear about which age group you are writing for. If you have what you think is a good idea for a children's book, then write to some publishers enclosing a brief outline (two pages should be enough). They may well be interested.

Genre Fiction

A great many writers specialize in writing a particular kind of popular fiction: crime, romance, historical romance, thrillers, science fiction, westerns – the categories are familiar to us all. Many of these occupy whole sections of the library shelves, and bookshops often have small departments dealing exclusively with one genre. Fashions come and go in genre fiction; for example, at time of writing there has been a vogue in the UK for mystery novels set in Ancient Rome, while the market for westerns has all but dried up. Overseas, the story may be quite different. The popularity of historical sleuths, from Cadfael to Sherlock Holmes and Philip Marlow, is almost universal, as is that of crime-fighting, or rather crime-solving detectives (pick any letter, say M for Maigret or Morse).

If you have an interest in writing for one of these categories, all of which are highly competitive, I would advise reading a number of books from each one. You will see that many are written to a formula, and strict rules often apply. The easiest example is that of mass-market romances such as those published by Mills & Boon where the requirements include no genital contact, no four-letter words, introduce the hero at a particular point, etc. Harlequin Mills & Boon produce guidelines for writers and even an audio cassette, from which it is not difficult to deduce that they receive an enormous number of applications from would-be authors. They are, in fact, very discerning in what they accept. Some professionals scoff at this type of writing, even claiming that it is not really writing at all but 'painting by numbers', and indeed it is true that conventions exist in all genres, like the old adage that a murder mystery should begin with the discovery of a body. Regular readers in these fields expect certain things from a book, and it is easy to sneer at them for being conservative or unadventurous. But not everyone can read Proust, or even Dickens, and most writers cannot afford to be snobbish. In fact a number of 'serious' writers make a steady income from writing genre fiction, usually under a pseudonym (some employ several). It is also more fun to write than many may realize – the rules can be broken. And there are, of course, many who have become highly successful and respected for working in one particular field, and prefer it to all else. The brilliantly researched historical novels of Bernard Cornwell (creator of *Sharpe*) stand in their own right, and there are many other similar examples.

Not surprisingly, there are how-to-write books in these fields, which can be found in the library. You may find writing a historical romance or detective story a sheer pleasure, and if it pleases you it may also please a publisher. Research, as usual: if it is a crime thriller, find out who publishes them and write a letter telling them what your book is about. A good plot, action and a strong protagonist are fairly essential, as are a well-researched background and an awareness of the audience you are writing for. Some people find plotting very hard work, others revel in it. If you find that you are skilled in working out the twists and turns of, say, a thriller, then perhaps this form suits you. It can certainly prove lucrative, for the market is steady and sometimes vast. Crime thrillers published in the UK may end up being published elsewhere, translated into other languages and perhaps even made into films. We can all dream a little.

Non-Fiction

Those who are fortunate enough to have not only writing ability but also specialist knowledge of one sort or another are in a very good position, particularly if there is a niche in the market for a new book on, say, antique porcelain, or surfing, or the Crimean War. I have been badgering a relative for years, a man who is not only an expert angler but can write too, to get down to writing his own book on fishing. He explains, quite rightly, that there are a great many books on fishing already, and one must have something new to say. Once again, a little research and one or two exploratory letters to publishers may pay dividends. I knew a former lecturer in accountancy who wrote a book on statistics some decades ago. It filled a niche in the market and became a set book on college courses the length and breadth of the UK. Since then it has never been out of print and earns him a steady several thousand pounds a year. While going through his divorce, the same person was grumbling to his publisher one day about the lack of a handy, comprehensive book to help the average person through this difficult experience. The inevitable followed: they commissioned him to write one, which he did.

Some lateral thinking is required here. Even if you are not an expert on a particular subject, you may be able to research it well enough to write a book on it: people do this all the time. Book packagers (listed in *The Writer's Handbook*) commission writers to produce text for often lavishly illustrated works, and pay them a set fee (the writer is sometimes not even credited). This can be a steady living for so-called 'commercial writers'. Whatever you decide to do, I recommend you read Michael Legat's *How to Write Nonfiction*, or another competent how-to-write book. Of course, you should be realistic and choose a subject that is not too well covered. The converse also applies: avoid a topic that is too obscure and would perhaps attract only a very small readership. But having said that, a search of the local library shelves soon reveals books on the unlikeliest and most esoteric of subjects. If you are keen to explore a particular topic, look at as many books on it as possible and find out who publishes them (then look up the publisher in *The Writer's Handbook* and make sure that they still do so). If you can demonstrate a knowledge of the topic, and convince a publisher that there is room for a new book on it, they may well be interested in commissioning you, and you may not have to write the whole book first; two or three chapters and a well-thought-out synopsis (i.e. a chapter-by-chapter outline) are often enough. The publisher will usually do some checking around first, to make sure that a book covering exactly the same territory as yours is not already in preparation somewhere else. But if all goes well, you could receive a contract and a modest advance and find yourself at work on your non-fiction book. You may be surprised to discover how much you enjoy writing it.

Biography

Writing a biography is always, to some extent, a labour of love in that you must be passionate enough about the subject to be willing to live with him or her – even if deceased – on quite intimate terms, perhaps for years. Biography is not to be taken lightly: it requires a lot of hard work and careful thought, and is beset by pitfalls of various kinds. But biographies sell well and are popular with publishers and booksellers alike. Biographers can make a good living from their work, and many distinguished authors specialize almost exclusively in the genre. A well-written biography (whether sympathetic or not), with a clear understanding of its subject and the times in which they lived is a joy to read (viz. Richard Holmes on Shelley, for example, or Richard Ellmann's classic *James Joyce*).

This is not, however, a field which is normally open to the new or unpublished writer. Biographies are commissioned, perhaps from an established writer who has convinced the publisher that it is time for a new study of a particular figure. New material relating to that person may have come to light, as in 1928 when an American academic, Leslie Hotson, discovered the inquest report into the mysterious stabbing of Christopher Marlowe, prompting several books on the intriguing playwright. Sometimes a little-known figure is chanced upon as a potentially interesting subject. And of course, there is a whole industry devoted to the writing of biographies of living people, from politicians and generals to pop stars and footballers. This field is particularly hazardous, the possibility of lawsuits being just one problem facing the biographer. Many such books are written by journalists who have access to press files, photographs and other materials not usually available to the lay person. The inexperienced writer is advised to steer well clear. In any case, the biographies (more accurately in many cases, the hagiographies) of the famous have almost always been written already.

Once again, however, and at the risk of sounding too forbidding, exceptions do occur, and if you are burning to write the biography of someone who (as far as you know) is not already covered, then you can at least investigate the possiblities. If, for example, the person concerned is – or was – a relative who had an interesting life, and you have enough material to fill a book about them, you could begin writing it, perhaps between other projects. When you have written two or three chapters and can produce a chapter-by-chapter outline for the rest of the book, there is no harm in approaching a few publishers of biography (research, as usual). You must be able to convince them that (a) this person's life-story is interesting enough for people to want to read it and (b) that you are competent to write it. Even if they are not interested, you may like to write it anyway, for yourself or your family – a true labour of love.

Journalism

There are opportunities for writers to earn an income from writing articles and features for newspapers and magazines. Bear in mind that the majority of those who make a real living from this sort of freelance work have a journalistic background, and probably journalistic training. However, some publications do take contributions from people who are new to them. Careful research of the markets is needed. You must decide what sort of articles you can write, and on what topics. Then look at as many magazines in the field as possible (you can find their addresses and the names of editors in any writers' handbook). A friend who runs a course for writers in this field suggests the following approach:

1 Ring up the magazine and ask for a press pack, if they do one. Otherwise drop them a brief, polite letter asking if they will consider submissions from freelances (include a c.v. if you can produce one that shows you know something of the business). Ask what sort of pieces they are looking for, and what length (for example 1,000 words). You should have already deduced the general style of the publication.

2 Send them a short outline (less than a page) of the piece you want to write. Often it needs to be topical, and naturally you will slant it towards their kind of readership (they might send you a profile of their 'typical reader'). Check the rates that are listed in *The Writer's Handbook* and ask for a realistic fee. For, say, a 1,000-word article you should not normally accept less than about £200 (half payable on delivery, half on publication), though this varies depending on the circulation of the magazine and what they can afford. Their status is classified according to how much it costs to advertise with them; for example, on 1998 figures, over £5,000 per page (*Cosmopolitan, Woman's Own,* etc.) down to less than £500 per page (*The Big Issue* etc.)

3 If you are commissioned, make sure you deliver on time.

There are various other ways in which writers can diversify, some of which will appear later in this book. But one important field of endeavour may be considered now.

Teaching Writing Courses

George Bernard Shaw's famous adage that 'those who can, do; those who can't, teach' may be only too applicable to some of the people who run writing classes, which is very unfortunate. The phenomenon of the creative writing course has been with us, in this country at least, since the late 1960s, and they are everywhere. The community education programme in your area probably lists at least one. I have taught them in adult education centres in London, and in remote village halls in the West Country. Evening classes are sometimes regarded as the panacea for a whole host of ills: a way to 'get out and meet people,' or to 'find a new interest'. In many cases (before we become cynical), this actually works. For writers, however – both those who attend courses and those who teach them – the whole area is far more contentious. Some disdain classes, claiming that writing cannot be taught; others have benefited considerably from them. A lot depends on the type of class, the make-up of the group, and the person who runs it. More will be said about the pros and cons of joining a course later; we are concerned here with writers who may wish to supplement their income by teaching.

The all-encompassing creative writing class is in fact less common nowadays. Courses are often targeted at more specific groups (for example elderly and retired people), or deal with a particular aspect of writing. Some have optimistic-sounding titles like 'Writing for Pleasure and Profit'; others are more honest ('Writing for the Terrified'). Some make unrealistic claims in order to attract students, such as 'anyone can do it', which is quite simply untrue. This has partly come about because all adult education institutes, for financial reasons, have a minimum enrolment figure nowadays, so that unless, say, ten people sign up for your course it will not run. Gone are the heady days when you could have fun teaching a group of five or six committed individuals, knowing that the course would still run next term. Nowadays, it would not even get started.

Writers with teaching experience are well placed to put a course together if they wish, but in fact this is not essential. The real essentials are enthusiasm, willingness to help beginners and a working knowledge of the subject. You do not even have to be a published writer, though at some point you may well find yourself being asked the unanswerable question: 'If you can't get your work accepted, then what chance have we got?'

It is, in fact, relatively easy to start a writing class, provided there are not too many of them in your area already. You simply approach the local community education or adult learning tutor (the reference library will have addresses on file) and ask them. This should be done by the spring or early summer when they begin putting their autumn programme together. Research first, however; if there is a well-established course in the region already offering the same thing that you are proposing, yours will not get off the ground. Being too narrow is also counter-productive; a course in, say, play-writing only, may not attract enough enrolments. Some tutors like to give their course a catchy title, like 'Have Fun Writing' or 'Writing from the Heart'. Decide what sort of course you want to run, find out whether there is room for it and be prepared to be flexible if necessary. You would be well advised not to try bluffing. A student who has paid his or her enrolment fee expects you to know your field, and to advise them not only on writing, but on what to do with a finished work.

You will sometimes see advertisements in the local papers for new community education – which usually means evening class – tutors, but even if there aren't any you can still write in with a plan for the course you propose, explaining why you are qualified to run it. If all goes well you will be invited in for an interview, or rather an informal chat. This is your chance to show the community education tutor that (a) you know your subject and (b) you are confident about teaching it. If you have a c.v. (you should have one anyway) you will already have sent it in, but bring an extra copy in case they have lost the first one. For a position as a writing tutor, samples of published work are very useful indeed, and will go a long way towards inspiring confidence in you. If you don't have any, you may need to use a little imagination in terms of making the most of your limited credentials: 'My novel *Escape from Epping* was short-listed for the Phyllis Badger Memorial Prize in 1996' sounds a lot better than saying it has never been published. You are, after all, a writer, so be creative.

Nowadays adult or community education departments have begun to insist that all tutors hold some sort of teaching qualification. This will usually involve your going on a short, part-time course to get a basic certificate in adult education and you may be allowed to do this while already teaching (they will advise you). Most writers probably won't want to pursue this road any further than necessary. Many, as already mentioned, insist that writing cannot be taught at all, and that writing courses are only useful for technical matters like laying out scripts and how to approach the markets. But as one who more or less began a writing career by going to an evening course, I cannot overstate the value of a good group run by a wise and committed tutor. It may not teach one how to write (and the vast majority of people I encountered on courses were not, and never would become, writers), but it can provide a forum in which your writing develops, in which you hone your technique, gain confidence and learn a great deal about the actual business of writing.

The length of the course you run will depend on local requirements, but a weekly class of two hours' duration, extending over, perhaps, two terms, is common enough. You will know in advance whereabouts the course will be held, and on which evening. Details will appear in the college brochure, for which you will be expected to provide copy, usually a brief outline saying something like: 'This course is open to beginners and experienced writers alike. Come along and have fun discovering your creative potential. Only pen and paper required.' You may then be invited to a tutors' evening shortly before the term starts, at which you will receive a welcome from the head of the department, and will probably be given lots of confusing pieces of paper. It is at this point, surrounded by tutors who are teaching courses in cake decorating, A level Spanish, Yoga, or windsurfing, that the writer often begins to feel like a fish out of water, and wonders whether they have done the right thing.

Be reassured; assuming your course has achieved enough enrolments, and you can disguise your nervousness at the opening session, you will soon get into your stride and may find that you actually enjoy it. The people who turn up will be a mixed bunch, of all ages, types and from all walks of life. Some will never have written anything before in their lives; others may know more about writing than you do (needless to say, a fair amount of tact is required when dealing with them). Some will be very shy; others will put your back up in the first five minutes with their arrogance. Whatever their experience and aspirations, remember that most are probably as nervous as you are, and wondering what will be expected of them. Your main job is to create a supportive and sympathetic environment, whereby people lose their fear of bringing along pieces of work to be read out and discussed. The rewards of this can sometimes be staggering. But there is, of course, a down-side; you can become jaded and frustrated, yearning to be at home producing your own work. Depressingly, a common enough figure is the writer who makes a steady income running courses, and never writes anything.

Rather than commit yourself to running a regular class for the local authority, you may find the prospect of teaching a short course more attractive. There are many residential and short courses, in various locations and of varying types (those run by the Arvon Foundation are perhaps the best known). Many of these are run by established writers, sometimes quite famous ones, and the fees for, say, five days' tuition, with full board thrown in, can be generous. Some writers enjoy teaching these courses as a break from their normal routine, and in turn, their name is a strong selling point for the people running the course. If you have a track record of sorts there is no reason why you should not seek out people who run such courses and approach them, though you will find the climate competitive.

Tutors of writing courses vary in their approach. Many like to get everyone writing and bringing in work to read out as soon as possible. Some set exercises of one sort or another, either in the session or as homework. Whatever the students write, the tutor must try to be positive about it, to see the merits or potential merits of it, and perhaps to suggest ways of improving upon it. This, however, is not the place for instructing writers in how to teach. The writer who undertakes the running of a course or workshop for other writers (or in practice, mainly for would-be writers) must think carefully before making the commitment – for a commitment it is. You cannot simply decide after two weeks that this is not for you, and then give it up; for one thing, you have probably signed an agreement to teach for the duration. In fact, as time goes on you may begin to find the experience stimulating and rewarding in a variety of ways, though I for one hotly deny ever having stolen an idea from any of my students – such a thing would be highly unethical.

5
Staying on Course

I am assuming for the purposes of this chapter, that you have begun your writing life and are engaged on one or more pieces of work. You are learning to write regularly, to pace yourself, and are beginning to experience some of the delights as well as the difficulties of the profession. Be assured, there are dangers ahead of which you have, as yet, barely dreamed of. One well-known writer, whose name, of course, I forget, said that he always felt there was an ongoing conspiracy by the rest of the world to stop him from doing his work. Distractions and interruptions have been mentioned already, but there are other problems inherent in the job itself. How do you avoid them, and stay on your course?

Submitting Your Work

Agents

A good agent is a blessing, and can help your career enormously. They not only take a lot of tedious administration and marketing work out of your hands (leaving you free to produce the goods), but they may actually find work for you, or bring your work to the attention of markets you barely knew existed. In return for this they take a commission on sales of your work: the standard rate is ten per cent but many now ask for fifteen per cent and usually a larger commission from overseas sales. In the latter case it is often well worth it – how many writers would know who to approach in, say, America or Australia, let alone Japan? On the other hand, writers sometimes leave their agents for a variety of reasons, feeling, perhaps, that they are not being looked after properly or that they can make more money elsewhere. A good author-agent relationship is rather like a marriage: some last a lifetime, others are doomed from the outset. There are quite a lot of literary agents, mainly in London, and a useful list can be found in *The Writer's Handbook*. My first agent, to whom I had been recommended by a BBC producer, was not listed in the handbook I owned at the time. When I queried this later they explained that they had never had a single fruitful enquiry via this channel and had subsequently withdrawn their name (and saved themselves an annual fee). Be warned: agents are contacted by a depressingly large number of hopefuls and 'wannabes' who have written something and have unrealistic expectations of success. Not surprisingly agents have grown wary of this and have evolved various means of filtering out time-wasting approaches.

Before you contact an agent, be clear not only about what it is you want from them, but what you can offer in return. Agents themselves say that the longer you can hold off, the better; a promising writing career that has already borne fruit will be of more interest than if you have, as yet, had no success. However if you have written a potentially commercial piece of work – crime fiction, for example, seldom seems to go out of fashion – they may welcome your approach. But it is a waste of time sending the manuscript of your crime novel to an agent who looks after film and television writers exclusively, or your film script to one who handles authors of general fiction. Those listed in handbooks usually state what kind of work they deal with ('No poetry, plays, or children's fiction' is a frequently seen phrase), and they will also state whether they require a reading fee, a preliminary letter, or some sample chapters of your book in order to assess whether it is worth their time reading the complete manuscript.

Literary agents are in a much-maligned profession, sometimes being lumped together with other sorts of agents, often less scrupulous ones, who represent, say, actors, or variety performers. In fact, most literary agencies are well-established firms who care about their reputations. It costs them a considerable amount in overheads simply to keep a writer on their books, and if that writer is not selling anything, they are clearly making a loss. Some agents have stuck by their authors through many a bad patch; others, regrettably, seem to have a periodic clear out of their non-lucrative clients. They often have a regular list of writers on whose behalf they work hard, and a common rejection phrase in letters from agents goes something like: 'we regret that our list is full at the moment'. Occasionally, however, they will take on new people if they show promise, or they might agree to try and place a particular work that has sales potential, making no commitment to represent you beyond that. For television or film an agent is pretty essential. They are in regular contact with companies, usually with individual producers and commissioning editors, and know how to negotiate the considerable minefields, as well as doing things like tying up the complex paper work involved and vetting contracts. For radio and theatre an agent is not essential but can be a help; they are often able to negotiate higher fees on your behalf, or put opportunities your way. This applies across all fields, so that a television company, for example, wishing to produce a new drama series, may approach agents in its search for suitable writers to join the team.

Getting an agent is very difficult if you are an unknown. If you strike lucky and achieve success by some other means, not surprisingly agents may well come to you; they are, after all, in business, and business is always competitive. If you too think professionally before approaching them in the first instance, you are more likely to be taken seriously.

Publishers

If you have written a novel and believe it is good enough for publication, you may choose to bypass agents and submit your work directly to a publisher. These are also listed in good writers' handbooks, and a careful search will reveal the sort of publisher who might be interested in your book. Needless to say, before sending the typescript out you will do some research into which publishers to approach. Publishers specialize, and you should look through a writers' handbook to find those that might be interested in your type of novel. The usual method is then to send two or three specimen chapters with a synopsis. If the publishers think these promising they will ask to see the rest of the manuscript. You can also look inside the front covers of books similar to yours and see who has published them. It seems banal to point out how foolish it is to send, say, a romantic novel to a publisher who specializes in books on gardening or aviation, but submissions like this happen every day and, understandably, publishers have grown tired of it. They too have put in place certain safeguards, and you will sometimes see the phrase 'no unsolicited manuscripts'.

There are a vast number of publishers and it is often difficult for the new writer to know who to approach and how to go about it. A preliminary letter is essential and should be brief, polite and to the point, telling them who you are (i.e. whether you have had any previous success from your writing) and what you have written, along with its length (number of words, how many chapters there are). A short synopsis, no more than two or three pages long is usually required. Plays, incidentally, will almost never be considered for publication unless they have been professionally produced, and usually only if they have been a commercial and/or critical success.

I recommend a reading of Michael Legat's book *An Author's Guide to Publishing*, which describes the whole process and will save the newcomer from wasting a lot of time. There is, when all's said and done, no reason to be discouraged: publishers are hungry for new material and generally welcome intelligent approaches from writers.

Vanity Publishing

Whatever sort of writing you do, you are well advised to stay clear of so-called Vanity Publishers. You will sometimes see advertisements claiming 'stories wanted', or asking 'do you want your book published?', or inviting you to 'become a published writer'. The procedure is then, that having sent off your manuscript (and been surprised to find how readily it is accepted), you pay them a substantial fee and your book is published, or perhaps your story included in an anthology, at a small print run. And that will be more or less the end of it, for the book is neither marketed nor distributed. You simply receive your stated number of copies, perhaps with advice on how to sell them yourself (from a market stall?). The vanity part lies in your being able to show that you are a published writer, and technically you are. Unfortunately, the publisher is not one you will find listed in any handbook, nobody has heard of your work, it will not be reviewed anywhere, nor will it appear in any bookshop.

This must be a strange, unsatisfying condition to find oneself in, for you have not really crossed the Rubicon of being published; you have merely paid to be in print. A good book, as any real publisher will tell you, is always worth publishing – and they pay you, not the other way around.

Family

Enter once again, the Supportive Partner (SP). He or she has learned by now to allow you space, both literal and metaphorical, in which to write. SP should also be learning not to expect quick results. Perhaps you have already suffered a rejection or six. Probably you were plunged into despair for a while, before picking yourself up and remembering that all writers experience rejection, and you must either rewrite the piece and/or send it somewhere else, or get on with another project.

SP has probably observed your behaviour during this time and is beginning to evolve mechanisms for coping with it. But before you start to lean on your partner too much, do remind yourself that SP is only human, and nobody's patience is infinite. The divorce rate among writers must be one of the highest, up there with rock stars and convicted drug dealers.

This is not a joking matter. Living with a struggling writer (which can be any one of us, at some stage or other) can be very difficult and demanding, requiring reserves of patience, tact and stamina. Struggling writers veer between highs and lows worthy of a manic-depressive, and no doubt, some *are* manic depressives. Others take to drink; in fact the drunken writer is a stock figure of drama, and of high and low comedy from as far back as you care to look. Ben Jonson was as familiar with the type in his day, as Hollywood is now (an extreme example being the hero, for want of a better word, of *Leaving Las Vegas*). The tired cliché that all creative people are over-sensitive, even tortured souls who need constant attention and protection from the world persists. Unfortunately this has been true on so many occasions that one is hard-pressed to deny it. It is well-nigh impossible to explain the reasons for one's angst to a level-headed, rational person, except perhaps to say, with regard to our profession, that the act of writing is a very personal thing, dealing with the subconscious, drawing on your own memories, neuroses, fears and aspirations. We are all, at times, 'slaves to the self'. Though there are occasions when writing comes easily, much of the time it is in fact very difficult to do. One writer told me that she believes she is on the very edge of her sanity when she is writing. Many will describe the experience of 'living' a scene from their book or play as they write it, sometimes laughing aloud, weeping or banging the table in anger. It is as well, on these occasions, that there is no one else within earshot.

The wives, husbands and partners of experienced writers may have grown used to such behaviour, but for those who are only now discovering it, no doubt it is quite alarming. Those writers who live alone may be able to indulge themselves at their leisure, though if they wish to preserve their sanity they too will need to escape sometimes and interact with other human beings. Those with spouses, partners and families, however, must find ways and means of keeping their relationships healthy. Most writers need support.

I believe that true loners who are content merely with their own company are the exception rather than the rule. Many writers I have known are sociable, even garrulous people who will sit up talking all night if you let them (the result of spending too much time on their own). Whatever your nature, you must try to make time for others, especially those who are closest to you. This will probably involve setting aside 'quality time' (which all relationships need anyway), like when you go out and do the things you enjoy together. When they do go out, however, writers can end up talking about their work, which rather defeats the object. A wise counsellor may advise you to develop ways of keeping your work seperate from family life, of switching off and leaving it behind when you close the door of the workroom. Unfortunately, since writers work with the material they carry in their heads, this is sometimes impossible. The conclusion we must draw is that you will have to find a strategy.

If you have children it is often a great deal easier because they will set their own agenda. Involving yourself with them is a tremendous antidote to work, to be entered into whole-heartedly. Playing games or taking them out somewhere can take your mind off things and enable you to return refreshed. But whether you have children or not, you would be well advised to find an activity which is in total contrast to your writing. Physical things like sport of course, do not suit everyone – writers seldom jog. Many find working with their hands relaxing, like the playwright Arthur Miller who made furniture in his workshop. Another playwright closer to home, Nick Darke, who lives on the Cornish coast, goes out fishing in his boat. Writers I know indulge in a wide range of activities from swimming to playing bridge, from fell-walking to running children's drama groups. Walking the dog is a universal favourite, which some find helps them to think ideas through. A discussion on the subject of escaping from the desk follows in Chapter 6, but the point cannot be made too strongly that if you do not want to end up separated from your spouse or family, you must try and see things from their viewpoint and realize that now you are a writer, your behaviour patterns may be changing. It is very easy to become introverted, even self-obsessed, when you write for a large part of your time. You might, to put it bluntly, have begun acting like a pain in the neck, assuming of course that you were not one already. So make an effort to take the writer's hat off sometimes and become a partner, husband or wife, mother or father again. You will feel much better for it when you return to work.

Coping with Writer's Block

Dorothea Brande, in her book *Becoming a Writer*, offers exercises by which writers may free the creative side of the brain and 'unblock' themselves, and clearly these have helped some people. How-to-write books often have an obligatory section on writer's block; it has become another cliché, a sort of occupational hazard like athlete's foot. In fact, some refuse to believe that it exists and there are writers who claim they've never been blocked in their lives. They may however have less fertile periods when they can't seem to get much done. Anyone of course, whatever their job, can grow tired of it at times and lose interest, but writer's block is seen as a more specific condition, in which the hapless scribe sits down eager to work, yet simply can't write – nothing will come out.

If you are still new to the writing business and think you are experiencing a block, I suspect that it is more likely you have not yet found your optimum time for working, or have not got into your routine fully. Trying to write at a different time of the day or night, taking a break from the work (a day, or even a week), seeing a film, or going to a beach may be all that is required to get you back into it. If it persists, step back and look at what you are doing. Has the story, chapter, or scene of the piece you are working on 'gone cold' on you – in which case can it be shelved and returned to later? Have you begun to think it isn't working? One solution might be to show your piece of work to another writer for an opinion, though this is fraught with difficulties and many will not like to be asked. How strong is your friendship with them – will it survive their telling you that the piece is dreadful and should be abandoned? (Before taking that to heart, it might be wise to get a second opinion.) If all else fails, and you really are blocked over a sustained period (i.e. weeks or months), more drastic action is called for. Some recommend meditation as a means of clearing the mind. I do not lightly advocate hypnosis or therapy, but talking at length to someone sympathetic may be one answer.

A writer I know who underwent nine months of psychotherapy, was very afraid that the process would stop her writing; that if all her angst, pent-up resentment, frustration and 'unfinished business' were removed (as if such a thing were possible), she would have no emotional spur left, no deep well of feeling, no creative force to drive her: in short that her writing would dry up. In fact the reverse happened. Within a matter of weeks the therapy sessions had released a wave of anger and energy in her that had been suppressed for years, and she began writing with passion and, just as importantly, with purpose. She completed the best play she had ever written, based partly on her own 'unfinished business' from childhood, and it was eventually commissioned and broadcast on BBC Radio. Anger, it seems, can be a very creative force if suitably channelled, but it is not the only driving force. I am pleased to report that, many years on, the person concerned is still writing, and writing well.

I do not deny the existence of writer's block, whatever it is. Sometimes it seems to result from fear; perhaps fear of exposing one's work (in effect, oneself) to others, or fear of failure. Sometimes it is simply due to overwork. Anyone can be emotionally blocked in one way or another, and somehow the block must be removed, or at least skirted. A friend suffering from a post-viral depression found that he was unable to write the sort of long pieces he had done until then; instead, to his surprise, poetry began to emerge. So he wrote poems for a few weeks, simply to please himself and release his emotions. After a while, he was able to write stories, then one day he sat down to write a play and found that he was able to work at it in his old manner: the block had melted away. So will yours, if you face up to it and prepare to tackle it. Here are my own practical suggestions:

1 Stop trying to force yourself to write. Admit there's a problem, let go of your work and walk away from the desk.
2 Do something else: take a holiday if possible, alone if this is what you want. Otherwise, change your routine and spend time with other people.
3 Don't keep trying to return to the desk; wait until you feel ready to begin, no matter how long it takes.
4 Do a different sort of writing if it feels right, like confessional poetry, or a monologue. Nobody need ever see it and it may unblock you, or at least stimulate new ideas.
5 When you have finished the new piece of work, try and ease yourself back into regular writing, without putting yourself under any pressure and have a back-up plan of what to do with the rest of the day (or week) if it does not work out.

73

If you are a writer, you will write again eventually. Sometimes you can trick yourself, i.e. sit down when you hadn't planned on doing so, and start a sentence. You may be surprised at what follows. In the end, as Raymond Chandler put it: 'The only salvation for a writer, is to write.'

Finding Ideas

Sir Tom Stoppard, in a 1999 edition of the Radio 4 programme *Start the Week*, said that his biggest problem nowadays was finding things to write about. One could imagine writers' heads nodding in agreement all over the country. It isn't merely the fact that everything you think up seems to have been done already; sometimes your own personal well of ideas simply runs dry. By some means or other, it must be refilled.

Sooner or later, most writers find themselves being asked 'where do you get your ideas from?' It is another one of those questions that provokes a pained reaction, starts you muttering to yourself or drives you towards the bar. (John Cleese used to reply that he got his ideas from a lady in Basingstoke, which usually silenced the questioner.) Ideas are, however, a writer's raw material, and without them you are helpless. So, when you are short of something to write about, where *do* you start looking?

The answer is, of course, anywhere and everywhere, but that is not very helpful. I see four broad categories that are worth delineating.

1   *Personal History, Relationships, or Experience*

A writer's first novel, it has often been said, is the one they need to get out of the way before they really start writing properly. This is because so many first novels have been based on the writer's own life experience, which they were eager to describe or to 'write out': their unhappy childhood, idyllic seaside holiday, loss of virginity, painful divorce (insert your own particular favourite). While the autobiographical approach has produced many great classics, nowadays it can produce groans from agents or publishers who lament the lack of an adventurous spirit among many first-time writers. Even so, most of us plunder our own experiences at least some of the time, and some seem to recycle them in a different form or guise for book after book. Critics and commentators may refer to a writer's particular 'territory', for example that of middle-class suburban angst (of which there are many exponents).

I have already said that I would not advise writers merely to write about what they know. But of course, one's own experience is, after all, unique, so if you can use it in an interesting way I see nothing wrong with doing so. A writing tutor I knew employed an exercise that always produced results: she would ask each student to come up with some incident that had occurred before they were ten years old, and which still rankled. 'Unfinished business', with the emotion it produces, is, as we have seen a fertile field. Many writers, if only unwittingly, also base their characters on people they have known; indeed it is sometimes difficult not to.

Old letters, family photographs and mementoes are often very effective in stimulating ideas; talking to an older relative may be equally productive. But you may be surprised to find how soon your own life experience is exhausted when it is turned into fiction, which is why so many people have only the one book in them. For the next one, you may need to look further afield.

2   Other People's Experiences

The wider you cast your net, the better. The experiences of others, whether relayed second-hand, handed down to you by a relative, or merely heard as anecdotes can become your experiences, or those of your characters. It seems fairly obvious that if you talk to as wide a range of people as possible, you will hear things from time to time that may spark off ideas.

3   Chance or Serendipity

This may include anything from an incident witnessed, to things heard on the radio or television, or snatches of conversation overheard on a train or bus. If it engages you, it may be all you need as the basis for a story – the grain of sand in the oyster. Someone I knew wrote a film script which sprang initially from the most trivial, innocuous source. Lying on a sunny beach, his attention was caught by the behaviour of a couple some distance away. A young woman was lying in her swimsuit on a towel, while an older man stood behind her and slightly to one side, upright and motionless except for a muscle in his neck which twitched uncontrollably. Mulling this over, our writer imagined the attractive woman was the girlfriend of a rich and powerful criminal, and the man a bodyguard assigned to look after her, who had become hopelessly infatuated with his charge. From such small beginnings, a plot can grow.

4 Documentary Sources

Whether you wish to research something specific, or are merely trawling through sources in search of material, ideas are all about you. Newspaper articles are a potentially rich field, but the national papers deal mainly with big stories, politics and international events. The local press, on the other hand, can be full of human stories which are far more interesting for the writer's purposes. Court reports, arrests, disputes between neighbours, accidents – there is a tale behind every one of these (you will, of course, change the names of the participants). Magazine articles, non-fiction books, even a footnote on a page may set you on the trail of an incident or life-story that can be built upon or , expanded to make a book, play, or whatever. And my golden rule (probably not original, but I forget where I first heard it) is: 'never let the facts get in the way of a good story'. The writer must embroider, speculate, extrapolate: in short, you take the basic idea and do whatever you like with it. Nobody will appreciate your having stuck rigidly and scrupulously to the facts if the resulting work is weak, or implausible, or has an unlikely ending. True stories don't usually have neat beginnings or endings anyway; you must shape the material. 'Based on a true story' is often a good selling point, and the writer need not go into detail about how much of it is true.

You must – and gradually you will – develop antennae for potential stories. This means being open at all times to useful ideas from whatever source. Writers are usually magpies in any case, clutter-heads who mentally file away interesting bits of information, names, or snatches of dialogue. I used to keep a notebook in which I jotted such things down, but gradually I got out of the habit. How-to-write books, particularly those aimed at beginners, sometimes advocate keeping an ideas book, but many writers don't bother. Mine became an old box file into which I stuffed scraps of prose or dialogue, outlines for plots, newspaper cuttings, good titles (none of them ever used) and other things which seemed worth keeping at the time. In fact, I have hardly ever employed any of this material. An idea, if not developed soon, often goes cold on you; the excitement it provoked when it first occurred fades, and rarely reappears. Better to stay with something that arouses your interest and, if possible, start work on it.

If you are a new writer, perhaps in a quandary about where to look for ideas, the following may be worth exploring. They make interesting enough reading in any case:

(a) The complete works of Sigmund Freud. A writer friend insists that you need look no further for possible plots.

(b) *The Thirty-six Dramatic Situations* by Georges Polti. Polti analysed a large number of plays and attempted to classify the plots into categories such as abduction, crime pursued by vengeance, etc., though some of his subdivisions taken from classical models are, to say the least, tenuous; for example, situation 26e: a woman enamoured of a bull.

(c) Newspaper obituaries. These are sometimes collected and published in book form, for example, *Obituaries from The Times, 1971–75*, in which the obituaries are given in alphabetical order.

(d) *The Chronicle of Britain*, edited by Henrietta Heald is available in reference libraries and is part of a series which includes *The Chronicle of the World* and *The Chronicle of the 20th Century*.

(e) *The Encyclopaedia of Superstitions* by E. & M.A. Radford, edited and revised by Christina Hale.

(f) *Anthologies and collections of true stories.* An example taken at random might be *Medical Murders*, edited by Jonathan Goodman.

(g) Collected letters. A favourite of mine is *Letters to an Actress: The Story of Turgenev and Savina*, edited and translated by Nora Gottlieb and Raymond Chapman.

This list could, of course, go on indefinitely. If you follow your own areas of interest, looking especially at non-fiction sources, it is remarkable what turns up. All is grist to the mill. Before becoming too obsessed with the notion of ideas, however, we might bear in mind the late Stanley Kubrick's remark: 'Ideas are a trap . . . you must have a *story*' [my italics]. It is true that ideas are ten-a-penny, and an idea is, after all, merely a germ, or a building block. You have to develop it, flesh it out, hone it and create your own story. But if you can find a ready-made one, so much the better.

While there are always new stories to tell, or new ways of looking at old ones, there is, nevertheless, a lot of truth in the notion that everything has been done, and a genuine shortage of original ideas does exist, particularly in the field of dramatic writing (plays and scripts). Television, film and radio consume stories at a frightening rate, leading to the familiar accusation of scraping the barrel and, of course, forcing writers to look harder and harder for ideas, sometimes in the unlikeliest of places. While a lot of books, plays and films deal with events of the past, some editors get tired of receiving too much historical material and maintain that they want to see writers reflecting the 'now' in which we all must live. In recent years some writers have turned to science, the new frontier, as a potentially rich and relatively untapped source. The popularization of science has become a minor industry, and many readable books exist on everything from genetic engineering to deep space exploration. This is, of course, our future, and it keeps arriving with ever-increasing speed. You do not have to call it science fiction: much of it will be reality soon enough. As writer and director Stephen Gallagher (author of *Chimera*) has succinctly put it: ' "now" is not a fixed moment, but a fast-moving target'.

Other Writers: Blessing or Bane?

When I met the playwright Peter Terson his first words were: 'I hate meeting other writers!' While the warm handshake and the friendly grin may have belied the statement, there is some truth in his words; not simply because writers are by nature solitary creatures, but because they often prefer to avoid mixing with other writers.

Most of us, on occasion, appreciate a good grumble, a chance to bemoan our lot to like-minded souls. Polls show consistently that people who do stressful jobs are best able to keep going not by consoling themselves with the large salary or the company car, or even with the importance of the job they do, but through the help and support of their colleagues. One's fellow-workers *understand*, and writers are like anyone else in this respect. Only other writers, I have found, really know what you go through and what it all means. However, while some happily seek the company of their fellow-scribes, many steer well clear of them, like hang-gliders occupying the same airstream.

In the days when I was active in the Writers' Guild I met a number of sociable writers who enjoyed taking part in committees, forging policies and generally being involved in the business of a writers' organization. Others did the job more out of a sense of duty, being prepared to serve their time before standing down and letting someone else do their share. But there were a great many other members – the vast majority – whom one never saw at all; who never attended meetings, or corresponded, or made their presence known in any way except, presumably, when paying their annual subscriptions. 'Most writers,' a publisher once told me, 'hide in the country.'

I believe this is partly a myth; it is not only writers who like to live in the country. Writers are generally more in touch with the real world than people think. They are, in one sense of course, jobbing artisans in competition with each other whatever their chosen field, for there are simply more people writing and submitting material than there are opportunities for publication, broadcast, or production. But this is not the only reason that few professional writers, in my experience, have other writers as friends. We enter a grey area here, and I have no ready theories; I merely notice that writers tend to choose their company from other walks of life. I may be one of the exceptions that proves the rule however, for there are a number of writers whom I phone up and chat to from time to time, to whom I can grumble about some recent rejection or cavalier treatment, who console me simply because they remind me that I am not alone and that other writers are going through similar experiences, every day, all over the planet. Some now talk to each other via e-mail, others like to write letters (a lost art, in the view of many), and even those who live the most monastic of existences may secretly devour the latest issue of their newsletter when it arrives.

If you do not propose to live like a hermit, what then are the means by which you can keep abreast of developments in the writing world? There are four main options: you might join a local writers' circle, you may subscribe to a writers' magazine, you may attend writers' conferences, or you may join one of the national organizations, like the Society of Authors, or the Writers' Guild of Great Britain, or you may do any combination of these, perhaps all four.

Writers' Circles

You will find a list of writers' circles in *The Writer's Handbook* but this is not exhaustive; I am aware of at least one in my region that is not listed, perhaps because they call themselves a club. The local reference library should have details of those near you. Like most such groups, the one I know meets regularly and has a range of activities. Sometimes a guest speaker – this is a useful earner for the more experienced writer – will talk on some particular aspect of the business ('How to Approach the BBC'), or they'll hold a short workshop on a topic such as 'Plotting Your Novel'. The occasional celebrity writer (if he or she does not demand a huge fee) might come along, perhaps to talk about how they first got published, or translated into French and Turkish. Members read pieces of work out to get feedback and (hopefully) constructive criticism. Experiences are swapped and information is exchanged on everything from poetry readings and competitions to new publishers looking for submissions. If you consider yourself a professional and feel you have progressed beyond such matters, you may be right; certainly the majority of the membership of these organizations seems to consist of new and unpublished writers, of all ages. But others still go along, if only to socialize and keep in touch; it can, after all, do little harm, and may provide a stimulus of one kind or another.

The newcomer can learn a great deal from talking with those who have been writing for a long while, and if at times you hear little more than grumbles and cautionary tales, you should listen anyway. More importantly, having your story, poem, or dialogue read aloud by others and getting the reactions of people who are hearing it for the first time is invaluable, as is (generally) the criticism that follows. It is a fact that many are more adept at judging and commenting on other people's work than they are at producing their own, because, of course, they can be objective. Some of those with whom I attended writing courses in my early days never wrote a line, being there for other reasons, yet I learned an enormous amount from their comments on my work.

Writers' Magazines

In this area one should be a great deal more circumspect. Hardly a year goes by without the launch of some new publication for writers, sometimes targeted at a particular group (usually the unpublished or aspiring writer). As I write, my daily newspaper contains an advertisement for a new magazine for women writers, *Mslexia*. The first issue (apart from offering a mystery free gift) contains features on erotic writing, feng shui for your desk and how to write a sonnet. Most writing magazines offer a broadly similar format: articles on aspects of the business, interviews with professionals, reviews, competitions, small adverts and perhaps a markets section.

Most of these sound useful and may even be invaluable at times, but a word of caution: the quality of magazines for writers varies enormously.

I still receive mailshots from the publishers of a magazine I foolishly subscribed to for a trial period more than ten years ago. I was surprised to find, especially as this purported to be a publication no writer could afford to be without, that the articles were very badly written (nor had I heard of any of the authors). As a writer of radio plays, I was appalled to find that an article on writing for radio had obviously been penned by someone who had never been broadcast in her life. It contained every cliché I have heard and a few others besides, gleaned perhaps from a quick perusal of a few outdated how-to-write books. From a practical viewpoint it was all but useless. The writers' markets section consisted mainly of a listing of teen magazines and other publications which might or might not consider unsolicited articles from new writers. The whole thing was poorly produced and grossly expensive. Add to this the fact that, when I contacted my bank to stop the direct debit instruction I had been obliged to sign, I was told that the magazine had put through the debit the previous day, i.e. before the stated expiry date. Fortunately the bank honoured my request to cancel.

The reader of this book will hardly need my advice not to take out a subscription to any writers' magazine without first obtaining a copy. Usually these magazines are not available from newsagents but by subscription only. You can write to the publishers and offer to pay for one copy, or a back number at a fair price. If they refuse, they may have good reason: perhaps the quality of the magazine is as low as the one I have described.

The fact is that aspiring writers – who probably outnumber practising writers by a factor of ten to one – are vulnerable and often provide an easy target. The publishers of the kind of magazines I have described (some of whom seem to be based in rather odd locations) know this and cynically exploit hopefuls eager for information and advice on how to break into the business. By far the best writers' magazines in the UK, not least because they are produced by 'real' writers for other writers, are those published respectively by the Writers' Guild and the Society of Authors; both are sent free to members but can be subscribed to by non-members. The *Writers Newsletter* is issued six times a year and at time of writing costs £15 per annum (postage paid), and is available from the Writers' Guild. The Society of Authors' journal *The Author* appears four times a year and costs £24 per annum (it is thicker than the *Writers' Newsletter*). Mention of these two important institutions leads us naturally to the next section.

Writers' Organizations

The Writers' Guild of Great Britain developed from the old Television and Screen-writers Guild, which was formed along similar lines to the Screen-writers Guild of America, i.e. by and for scriptwriters. Gradually it took in every sort of writer and most recently amalgamated with the smaller Theatre Writers' Union, bringing several hundred playwrights under its wing, to produce a current membership of over 2,000.

The Guild is a trade union for writers, affiliated to the Trades Union Congress (TUC) but not to any political party (its members are of all shades of opinion). It carries out many activities but its paramount tasks are to help writers with their difficulties (for example, giving legal advice), and to negotiate agreements and codes of practice on behalf of writers. Working parties deal regularly with bodies like the BBC, the Independent Theatres Council (ITC) and the Producers Alliance for Cinema and Television (PACT). There are numerous committees involved in every area of writing, from radio, television, film and books, to the women's and young media committees. Apart from a permanent full-time staff, the Guild has an executive council of elected representatives who meet regularly to formulate and implement policy, hear reports, monitor developments in all areas and generally oversee business. The committees meet individually and report to the executive council.

The membership is very wide ranging, from famous names who pay their subscription even though they may take no active part in the Guild, to first-time writers just beginning their careers.

Membership used to be open only to those writers who had had work published, broadcast, or produced in the professional theatre and could show documentary evidence to that effect (for example a contract). There was an exclusive points system by which a full-length play or script gained twelve points, and so on, and only writers who had clocked up the requisite number were admitted. In more recent years, recognizing that it must move with the times and that writers' organizations need to be stronger than ever nowadays in an increasingly complex, competitive and often hostile climate, the Guild has slackened its entry rules and introduced a new category of candidate membership for unpublished writers. There were, and no doubt still are, a large number of potential members out there who could make a contribution, as well as increasing the subscription income. At present the minimum annual subscription for full members is £100, but this increases as a percentage of the writer's income if it rises above certain levels, i.e. those who earn most, pay most.

The Society of Authors is much older than the Guild, having been founded by George Bernard Shaw and others in 1884 'to protect the rights and further the interests of authors'. It has a prestigious reputation: its first president was Lord Tennyson (the current one is P.D. James). Its activities are broadly similar to those of the Guild and it too is now a trade union, though not affiliated to the TUC. The Society has over 6,000 members, more of them in the field of books, both fiction and non-fiction, than those of the Guild, though the Society contains writers working in all areas. It is in the enviable position of owning the rights to the works of various authors (such as G.B. Shaw who bequeathed them to the Society) and so has additional incomes to its subscription revenue. The Society has a management committee of elected members who serve for three years, and a full-time staff. It also administers various awards and distributes large sums in prize money each year. It has a system of associate membership for writers who are not yet published but can show evidence that they will be; as with the Guild, full membership requires evidence of professional credits. The Society also publishes pamphlets called 'Quick Guides' on various topics (income tax, VAT, etc.) which are free to members, but can be purchased by non-members. It has a fixed rate of subscription, currently £70, payable on application, but writers under thirty-five who are not yet enjoying 'a significant income' from their writing may apply for a lower rate of £52 per annum.

Writers' Conferences

Whether or not you commit yourself to joining any group or organization, some writers' groups and circles, as well as various other bodies, organize writers' conferences. They are normally open to anyone who can afford the fee, which may or may not include things like refreshments and, if it is a residential affair, accommodation. These events are held at a range of locations and vary considerably, from half-day gatherings that are sometimes thinly disguised recruiting sessions to attract new members, to full-blown festivals lasting a week and boasting celebrity guests by the barrow load. Some of the latter events, however, are of little use to writers (except as paid speakers) but are patronized in large numbers by readers, eager to hear their favourite crime writer speak, or a famous poet interviewed. There are sometimes optional workshops alongside the main programme, on various aspects of writing, but again these are likely to be attended by interested laypeople and dilettantes rather than by writers. Writers, by and large, are at home working.

Conferences that are organized by writers themselves usually have less hullabaloo about them and tend not to be widely advertised, with listings appearing in publications like the *Writers' Newsletter*. One that I helped to organize, which is probably fairly typical, was a one-day event at a medium-sized centre in Bristol. We booked a conference room for the day, seating up to around fifty people. As speakers, in the morning session we had the writer-in-residence of the Bristol Old Vic Theatre, followed by a BBC Radio producer. In the afternoon we had a television writer from a famous soap opera followed by an established author whose new novel had just been published. Hence the areas of theatre, radio, television and books were covered, with ample time left for questions and discussion after each speaker had talked about their work. There was also a final session by a representative of the Writers' Guild – we made no bones about recruiting. There was a good café and plenty of convenient space for writers to chat informally (somewhere for smokers to go is also an advantage at writers' conferences).

Attending such gatherings can not only take the sting out of one's lonely existence, it can be a way of picking up ideas and making contacts; of (that awful word) *networking*. Writers are often very bad at this kind of thing (which is why they have agents); we are not, by and large, natural salesmen and saleswomen, or even natural mixers. However, a little effort to mix may well pay off: a chance conversation at a theatre conference I attended led me to work (briefly) with a director at the Royal Shakespeare Company. And, of course, hanging around the bar can be very rewarding. As the evening wears on, you may be staggered at whom you find yourself in conversation with – not that they are likely to remember you the next morning, even if you remember them. But whatever your experience of the event overall, you will probably return to your work the richer for it.

6

Escaping from the Desk

Following on from the matters mentioned in the previous chapter, there is a serious occupational hazard for writers which demands special mention. After working alone for some length of time, writers may easily become stale, needing stimulus, or at least a recharging of the batteries. After writing for a longer time they can become out of touch, which is even more dangerous. The sad figure of the isolated, ageing writer in his book-lined study, still reworking the same material that made his name thirty years previously, is not without foundation. But since few of us can afford to take frequent holidays, how can we remain fresh while still working? The following selection of possible remedies is not, of course, exhaustive; writers' needs vary enormously. Nevertheless, it should provide some helpful starting points.

Collaboration

Writers have probably collaborated since the earliest times. The Elizabethan dramatists had no qualms about working in pairs, or even adding bits to other people's plays (this was before the laws of copyright). Much of this kind of writing was, admittedly, hackwork. Professional writers were hired quickly to rewrite or spice-up a weak script, usually at a penny a line. Much later, Hollywood did the equivalent (look at the number of screen-writers credited on *Casablanca*). Writers have frequently paired up to write for radio and television, and books too, though this is far less common. We can all name famous British comedy-writing duos, from Frank Muir and Dennis Norden, through Galton and Simpson to French and Saunders. Such relationships can become as intimate as a marriage as the two writers mesh together, not just personally but stylistically. Barry Took has described his successful partnership with the late Marty Feldman as being so close, he often felt their scripts were written by a third person named 'Barry Feldman' or 'Marty Took'. Many such teams, so the cliché goes, consist of a pacer and a sitter, meaning that one paces the room thinking up things while the other types, throwing in suggestions along the way. Of course, ways of working together simply evolve over time, and partners develop one which suits them best. John Cleese and Connie Booth, while writing *Fawlty Towers*, would take a huge sheet of paper and sit at opposite sides of it. One would then write a word or fragment, the beginnings of a plot, and the other would look at it, and on their end of the sheet write something that then occurred to them as a result. Gradually, moving closer together, they would add words and phrases until eventually they had covered the sheet, and there they would have the basis of that particular episode. Of course, the two knew each other very well (they were, after all, married to one another). Their method may seem bizarre but it produced excellent results.

My favourite example is that of a system I was told about, which may be apocryphal. In America in the 1940s, teams of radio comedy writers, under pressure to write fast and funny, are said to have employed the 'whiskey and rubber band' method. The writers would sit round a table, with a glass of whiskey in the centre. Every one of them had a rubber band around his head. In turn, each would suggest a gag. If the others laughed, it was a success and the writer got a drink of whiskey. If it was a dud, someone would reach out and snap the rubber band against the unfortunate scribe's forehead as an encouragement to do better, before the next one took his turn.

There are, of course, less painful ways of collaborating. If you know someone with whom you feel you have enough rapport, you may want to approach them with a view to working together.

Naturally you must share similar aims, respect each others' writing ability and be able to trust one another. On the one occasion I collaborated with another writer (on an outline for a radio comedy series), I was gratified to find not only how much I enjoyed the experience, but how quickly we got things done. It was, simply, a lot more fun than working alone. We would sit in my kitchen, and after an initial coffee and some small-talk we'd begin throwing ideas around, sometimes laughing aloud, sometimes scribbling things down. The plot took shape, often by a process of elimination: 'No, he can't say that because his wife doesn't know he's leaving his job. He'll have to tell a lie. And since he's a terrible liar, he'll get himself into further trouble . . .' etc., etc. Since we knew the setting and characters well, we soon found story-lines to suit them. We laid down some simple ground rules at the beginning, similar to the ones used by Dali and Buñuel when they wrote together (my colleague was a film buff). Paramount was the rule that if one of us didn't like an idea it was rejected without further discussion, lest it developed into an argument and thence to a bone of contention. Of course, others might do it differently; some thrive on adrenalin and enjoy hammering out ideas through passionate argument. It can, in some circumstances, be stressful: the writers' room during the hectic run-up to recording of the BBC Radio 4 satire show, *Week Ending*, was often a hotbed of fraught tempers and bruised egos.

Whether you collaborate or not depends largely on the kind of work you are doing. Clearly, a novel or story (let alone a poem) is a personal matter and not likely to benefit from teamwork. Dramatic writing is better suited to being written by pairs of writers, who can construct dialogue together. When it comes to plotting, which is to a large extent a technical matter, two heads are often better than one; one can suggest ideas while the other points up weaknesses and offers alternatives. From time to time you can switch roles, the other one then playing devil's advocate, and so on. Some fields of endeavour are almost certain to require collaborators with particular skills, the most obvious one being that of the musical. While there are a very few extremely talented people who can write not only the story and song-lyrics, but the music too (Stephen Sondheim, for example, or Willy Russell), most musicals are created by a team made up of composer, lyricist and perhaps others, for example, a separate story-writer). To deal adequately with the subject of musicals would require a whole book at least; I suggest anyone interested starts with *Writing a Musical* by Richard Andrews.

For writers to collaborate it is not even essential that they meet face to face, though this would seem desirable from time to time, at least in the early stages of developing a piece of work. People may now communicate via e-mail and some famous musical-writing partners apparently work independently, coming together only at agreed intervals to play through what they have done. However, this really applies only to experienced writers who have probably worked together before and know each other well. For the fairly new writer, collaboration is quite a bold step to take. Those embarking upon it must tread carefully. If, for example, one partner emerges as the dominant figure, that may work well so long as the other is happy to take the more submissive role. If both are striving for dominance there is tension, but that, of course, can be highly creative and can produce results. As we have seen it is all rather like a marriage: it may end in failure, but one should at least be able to learn something from the experience.

If you want to work with another writer yet do not know anyone suitable, you can advertise, though this involves a serious element of risk. One sometimes sees advertisements in, for example, *The Stage & Television Today* for a comedy writing partner wanted, or a lyricist. Often whoever it is may live far away, which produces obvious logistical problems. Even if they are within reach, the chances of the chemistry being right between you are, it has to be said, somewhat slim. Writers may avoid this problem by being specific about what they want; for example, 'Scriptwriter, forty, radio and TV experience, *Father Ted* fan, seeks similar to develop whacky new sitcom idea. London area. Send c.v. and samples of your work to Box No. . . .' etc. Many try to cast their net wide, perhaps advertising over several weeks and in different places, then sifting through a large number of replies to find one that sounds right (comparisons with lonely hearts adverts are obvious). Luck, of course, plays its part, and more than one set of successful writing partners have met through an advertisement. You should be clear about what you want to do, and then search for someone who shares your views, aspirations and hopefully your vision too. When it works, the rewards can be immense.

Writer-in-residence Schemes

For the Year of the Artist, i.e. 2000, the Arts Council is providing a large sum of money to fund, via the regional arts boards, a hundred artists' residencies in all parts of the country. In fact, allowing writers to escape from their desks and operate in various environments for a fixed term, is a practice with a rich and varied, if relatively short history. The places in which such residencies have been set up range from the conventional to the bizarre. The Millennium Dome has its writer, universities sometimes have them, as do prisons, hospitals and hospices, schools and colleges, even (for a while) the BBC. The poet Tobias Hill was for a time a resident writer at London Zoo; another I heard about was based on a North Sea trawler.

Whether these placements constitute a serious contribution to the arts and to the community, or whether they merely serve as 'nice little earners' for professional writers is a matter of some debate. Residencies vary enormously; some have been undoubted failures on one side or both, others resounding successes. The degree of success depends on such factors as a set of clear aims and objectives from the appointing body, realistic expectations on both sides, choosing the right writer for the post and motivating him or her to do their best. Potentially, spending time as a writer-in-residence can be a wonderful experience. Whatever its outcome, however, you will be paid for a fixed term to be somewhere else, which is probably no bad thing in itself.

Since the 1970s there have been occasional advertisements in the press under the arts and media sections for writer-in-residence posts, perhaps at a university or attached to a theatre. The writer would probably be hired for a year and expected to fulfil a number of functions, from running a young writers group or a series of poetry workshops, to writing a new piece of work specially for the institution concerned. Usually these posts are only open to experienced, professional writers, particularly those whose name would add clout to the institution and help its publicity. During the 1980s, HM Prisons also began hiring writers to work with inmates, and have continued the practice. Not surprisingly, these are among the most difficult placements, leaving some writers with harrowing tales to tell, but providing most with the opportunity of learning a lot from their time at a prison, and feeling they have even done some good. Having been interviewed for such a post, I am unlikely to forget the experience, when, as one of a group of six writers, I was shown around a category C prison, a grey, Victorian fortress which still had the stone bays where convicts once picked oakum.

Nowadays, with a general lack of funding available (aside from particular initiatives such as the Year of the Artist), it has to be said that writers' residencies are few and far between, and when a post is advertised there is a deluge of high-calibre applications for it. The new, or even the published writer will find himself or herself competing with seasoned professionals eager for a funded post, in effect a year off from their other work. However, with the arrival of the National Lottery, there are, in theory at least, more funding opportunities now than there have ever been, and here the writer may need to be proactive rather than merely reactive. In other words, you may be able to set up a residency yourself. You would need to look around and seek out an institution – for example a local university department, community college, library, or hospital – which is interested in having a writer work with them in one way or another, and then make a joint approach via the Arts Council's lottery department. The local regional arts board should be able to advise you. Bear in mind that competition for every kind of arts funding is very fierce, and your project may never get off the ground. But if you relish the idea of working in a different environment for a while, it may be worth exploring.

My own experience of doing a short residency was a pleasant one. Funded by the Arts Council's Arts for Everyone scheme (now, alas, defunct), I worked for a few months with a drama school and wrote a radio play for students, which was recorded and broadcast on BBC local radio. This involved working with the students on the script at weekly sessions, alongside their voice tutor, and exploring the art of radio acting. Not only did I get away from the desk, I was in a bustling environment that was new to me, working with other talented people; it was a rewarding and enriching experience.

Community Plays

For playwrights, the chance to write a community play may come along only once in a lifetime, but those who have taken on this mammoth task and seen it through, will have been through a unique experience that will change them forever.

Community plays as we know them were more or less invented by the playwright Ann Jellicoe in the 1970s. From her Dorset home she began working first with schools and then with a wider range of local people, and produced plays in which a whole community could take part, and in which casts of 150 or more were common. From these beginnings, the phenomenon has grown to the point where community plays take place all over the country, as well as overseas, in towns, cities and villages. There are organizations like the Colway Theatre Trust, founded by Ann Jellicoe, which go into communities when invited and help them put their play on. There is a professional production team, and usually a professional writer is hired to write the play, often to given requirements, which might be, for example, to tell a story the community have researched themselves from local history sources. The whole thing will take a year or more, from its initial concept to its performance, which may take place in the open air, or in some large indoor space. Many playwrights, from unknowns to famous names, have written community plays and are the better, both personally and professionally, for having done so. Some do them on a fairly regular basis, but for most writers the opportunity to find such work is rare.

Community plays have been labelled 'theatre on the cheap' or 'amateur dramatics posing as art', being looked upon as an activity in which professionals manipulate large numbers of bedazzled amateurs for a few months under the guise of creating worthy theatre 'by and for' the community. My own experience of writing a community play belies that view. It was heady, intense, infuriating in some ways, humbling in others. Certainly it was unlike anything else with which I have ever been involved. The standard of acting varied, but it was both gratifying and moving to see people who had shown up on the first day nervous and lacking in confidence, turning in exciting performances. By the end I felt that all who had taken part in the process were, as I was, enormously enriched by the experience.

The advantages of the brief are obvious to any playwright who, in the financial climate of today's professional theatre, is frequently told 'one set only, and a maximum of three actors'. Here, there are *no limits* on the size of the cast, on their age, sex, or anything else; *no limits* to the number of sets, or costumes, or to the play's scope for music, song and dance. If I wanted a brass band (which I did), or fire-eaters, or wrestlers (which I did) I could have them. The prospect of such freedom comes to the writer like a banquet to a starving man.

As may be imagined, writing for a cast of a hundred people or more, of all ages, many of whom have never acted before, calls for not only a strong imagination, a fair amount of skill and an awareness of theatrical techniques, but also reserves of patience and stamina. The subject requires far more space than I can devote to it here, but the interested writer might do well to start by seeing one or two community plays and perhaps reading Ann Jellicoe's book *Community Plays: How to Put Them on*. If you hear of a play being planned in your area, it may be worth making contact with the steering committee at once because often they prefer to use a local writer, with local knowledge, rather than 'parachuting in' an established professional (who will probably want a higher fee too). But it should be stressed that writing a community play is not a job for the outright beginner.

Writing for Amateur Theatre

If money does not constitute a problem for the present, and you like the idea of writing a play for local performance, you might make contact with an amateur theatre company (start by obtaining a copy of *The Amateur Theatre Yearbook*, perhaps from your local library). In recent decades the vast majority of such groups have shaken off the tired, village hall image of wobbly sets, tacky costumes and appalling acting. Go along to a performance at the local amateur theatre and you may be surprised at how high the standard is, not to mention how bold the choice of play. The old stock repertoire of Noel Coward and Terence Rattigan has given way to an enormous range of pieces, from musicals, pantomimes and comedies, to the works of some of the most challenging and controversial of today's serious playwrights.

Some of these amateur companies are open to the idea of a new play being written for them. Of course, they will be unable to pay a proper fee, though perhaps some expenses may be covered. However, the advantages for the writer, as with community plays, may be considerable: a large, enthusiastic and committed cast who are doing it for the love of performing; good, sympathetic audiences, and the chance to mix with a range of people from many walks of life, who value your contribution. This can be a good place for the new playwright to start out; you have a ready-made showcase for your play, to which you can invite theatre professionals such as directors or literary managers. But be warned: they will offer any excuse not to come. Many of them are snobbish about amateur theatre anyway, an attitude which I have found unjustified, having seen better acting in some amateur companies than on the stage of the local professional theatre.

If the company balks at the idea of taking on a new play, they might be interested in a pantomime. For many, the all-too-familiar range of Christmas standards has become jaded, and there is room for brighter and more up-to-date pieces. A number of villages in my region stage their own pantomimes, written by someone they know, full of in-jokes and local references. The writer can have a lot of fun doing this, provided you keep it all in perspective and do not have expectations of material reward (or of very good acting; these are not usually amateur actors from a company, but ordinary folk having a go). Writing comedy, from gags, puns and quick exchanges to physical, knock-about stuff, is good practice for the writer who is still learning the craft of theatre writing, and often a breath of fresh air to busy professionals who wish to put aside their regular work and go completely over the top for a while. You may be slightly surprised to learn that there is even a market for pantomimes, a few writers having made a living from them and earned respectable reputations.

Travel Writing

For those who really want to escape, not just from their workroom, but further afield, travel writing of one sort or another may provide an answer. If you are a published writer you might try to interest a publisher in a book about a place you intend to visit, or an interesting journey you want to make. Extensive research in this field is essential – not just into who publishes the sort of book you want to write, but into those books that already exist, as the place may have been covered more fully than you expected.

The market here would seem to be healthy, as there are many armchair travellers who love reading about places they themselves cannot or will not visit. Some travel writers have indeed become household names, and not only those who have featured on television. Before getting too excited about the idea however, bear in mind that publishers receive a great many approaches from people who think that this is an easy way to make money from simply taking a holiday. *Wanderlust* magazine apparently receives about 300 unsolicited articles a month, half of them from people who do not appear even to have read the magazine.

My namesake, the explorer and travel writer John Pilkington (no relation), says that he goes away to *save* money, as it is often much cheaper to live in remote parts of the world than it is to stay in England. He rents out his house while he is absent and spends several months travelling, taking photographs along the way and keeping a detailed notebook, in which he not only records things like names, dates and impressions, but sometimes writes whole passages that will appear in the final book. On his return to the UK he writes it up. In the early 1980s, having already contributed articles to travel magazines, he made plans to visit Nepal for his first major trip. About nine months before setting off, having researched the market thoroughly, he started approaching publishers with detailed proposals, carefully tailoring each one to suit their list. Within a few months he had received some interested responses as well as some helpful recommendations. The book of that trip, *Into Thin Air*, was eventually published by George Allen and Unwin in 1985; in fact, he was determined to make the trip with or without a publisher – the mark of a true traveller. In the event, each of his three travel books to date have ended up being commissioned before he left the UK, and a portion of the advance therefore helped to finance the project (a writer's advance is often paid by a publisher in stages, i.e. partly on signature of the agreement, and partly on delivery of the manuscript). A word of caution here, however: no publisher is going to pay an advance unless they have confidence in the writer's serious intent and ability to produce the book. If you can already demonstrate your skills (for example, with published articles) this is a big advantage. Another one is the ability to take your own photographs of publishable quality.

In John Pilkington's view there are still many parts of the world to write about (Siberia is just becoming known), as well as new things to say about more familiar places. However, he advises would-be writers of travelogues to examine their motives: are they travellers who want to write, or writers who want to travel?

Travel Guides

It is obvious from a visit to any library or bookshop that there are an enormous number of travel guides published. This is a potential earner for writers, since travel guides become out of date and new ones are needed from time to time. It is also, of course, a competitive field. There are many publishers of such books, ranging from small presses to the giants. Some guides are low-budget affairs, poorly produced, and the writer is advised to steer clear of those who publish them. Others are lavishly illustrated, packed with detailed information and well written, often by a team of contributors. Some of them are writers with a journalistic background;

others combine writing with photography, while others still are people who may have specialist knowledge of a particular country or region. As always, do some research and see if you can identify a niche in the market.

Travel Bursaries

If you want to travel, and not necessarily to write about it (or not immediately anyway), you may investigate other ways of getting funded. There are various possibilities, from private sponsorship to fellowships and bursaries. The travelling fellowships offered annually by the Winston Churchill Memorial Trust are a well-known example. They make one hundred awards to people from a wide range of backgrounds, who are able to 'show that they can make effective use on their return to this country of the knowledge and experience they have obtained abroad'. The Trust issues a brochure available from libraries which specifies particular professions and categories of people who are eligible to apply. This may or may not include writers; it varies each year. The number of applicants is, of course, huge, so a well-researched and well-thought-out application is essential.

The Society of Authors awards travelling sholarships annually (to the value, I believe, of around £2,000) to British authors wishing to travel abroad. 'Bursaries, Fellowships and Grants' are listed in *The Writer's Handbook*. As always, further investigation may bear fruit.

There are, of course, other ways by which the writer might escape.

If you have a friend or relative who will loan you their holiday cottage for a few weeks, perhaps out of season, you are luckier than most. And after all, if you own a laptop computer you can work anywhere, outdoors, or in some remote mountain cabin. Other writers have found it useful to go on one of the short brain-storming courses which are occasionally advertised, run perhaps by one of the so-called 'writing gurus' who have made a name for themselves (c.f. the screen-writing courses mentioned in Chapter 3). But wherever you go and whatever you do, it is important to try to refresh yourself now and then, before returning to the struggle.

When you do return, you may find yourself having an experience common to more or less all writers – that of opening the front door and seeing, in the pile of mail on the mat, an envelope that you recognize at once for what it is: a rejection. Welcome home, and read on.

7

Coping with Failure

'I think that to do good work in any of the arts you should be scared every day.'

André Previn, interviewed in the *Radio Times*,
October 1984

Working with nothing but your mind and whatever you can extract from it and shape into a workable form takes courage. It can be very hard work, it is at times frightening and of course no one thanks you, or even respects you for doing it, unless you become visibly successful. Writers sometimes have a reputation for being whingers who are never satisfied and think the world owes them a living. This disparaging attitude towards us is particularly notice-able in Britain, in spite of (or perhaps because of?) the fact that this country has probably the richest literature in the world, from Shakespeare and Milton to Dickens and Eliot *et al.* Go further afield – to France or Ireland, to name only our nearest neighbours – and you will soon discover that writers are generally treated with a much greater degree of respect. A talent for writing is recognized as something precious, needing nurture and encouragement. Hence it is difficult to accept that your efforts, particularly early on in your career, will often meet with failure. Rejection is some-thing you will have to deal with at all stages of your writing life. Whole books could be written on it; we must be content here with rather less.

How to Handle Rejection

When it comes to receiving rejection letters you are in distinguished company, for virtually every writer has had them. John Osborne's famous work *Look Back in Anger*, the landmark play of the 1950s, was rejected by every agent and theatrical management he sent it to before the Royal Court Theatre, the sole champion of new writers at that time, took it on board. Its success since then is legendary. Four decades later, little seems to have changed; Paul Godfrey's play *Inventing a New Colour*, a minor success of the early 1990s, was turned down by every theatre except the very last one he tried – the Royal Court. Literary history is strewn with such tales, and every writer you are likely to meet will have a stock of them. Most common are those instances of publishers who knocked back a novel time and again, which eventually found its way into print and ended up being a bestseller or winning an award. Agents have quite often regretted rejecting people who went on to become successful, as those record companies must have done in the early 1960s when they famously turned away a young Brian Epstein seeking a contract for his protégés, the Beatles.

An example from my own experience is fairly typical. When I began sending out a stage play I had written in 1993–4, the range of responses I received from various theatres, literary managers and agents was enormous. Looking through the rejection letters, you would be excused for thinking that they were not all talking about the same play. Some hated it, others saw merit in it but felt that it was not good enough to reach production, while one or two, thankfully, expressed interest. The play was in fact taken on by a small, touring theatre company with which I had already worked. As part of a local new writing season, they gave it a rough, platform producton for two nights (i.e. without set or special costumes), and, after a favourable audience response and a review in the *Guardian*, commissioned it for full production the following year. The play toured for several months and ended up transferring to a respectable London fringe theatre. A very satisfying moment for me, was when it played for a week in one particular theatre – which shall remain nameless – whose literary manager had turned it down the year before with very negative and discouraging comments. I do not know whether he went along to see a performance; probably not.

The conclusion we may draw from all of this is that the powers that be are not, of course, infallible. Their opinions are subjective and are influenced by a range of factors including personal taste, commercial considerations and sometimes a plain lack of insight. Literary managers, for example, are not well paid, even in the larger theatres, and while the majority are no doubt men and women of talent and integrity who do their best to assess the work sent to them and to encourage writers of promise, others are biased, conservative and even incompetent (sometimes all three). One or two – perhaps more than one or two – are embittered, burned-out, or failed writers themselves, who privately think they have more right to be getting their work commissioned than you or I have.

Whatever the reasons for a piece of work being turned down, however, the writer must accept, to some extent, that rejection is par for the course. Often, it must be admitted, manuscripts are rejected for perfectly good reasons, and unfortunately the writer is the only one who cannot or will not see them. Over-confidence is as dangerous as lack of confidence. But sometimes, a rejection appears to have no logic behind it at all. The agent, publisher, script editor or literary manager concerned may in fact have sound reasons, of which you are unaware, for not being able to take an otherwise good piece of work any further; for example, the budget is tied up for a long time ahead, or a decision has been taken at senior level not to commission any more prison dramas, or detective stories, or historical pieces, or post-feminist novels (add your own category). As we have seen elsewhere, a sensitivity towards the market is essential for the writer, whatever field they are working in, and a few preliminary enquiries may save a lot of heartache and wasted time.

Most rejections, however, still come as a shock, and it would be dishonest of me to say that one gets used to it; one does not. You may gradually learn to live with it, but it still hurts, every time, even on those occasions when you have half-expected it.

I often believe that rejections make a special noise when the post-

102

man (in our street, the postwoman) pushes them through the letter-box. They land on the mat with a sound like the Crack of Doom (this is partly because the envelope containing your manuscript is usually heavier than anything else in the mail). Almost invariably, you recognize it at once because the address is in your own hand-writing and the envelope is the one you obligingly enclosed with your submission (in our house it is known as a BBE – big brown envelope). With sinking heart, you pick the fearsome thing up and retire elsewhere, perhaps back to bed, where you can hide for a while, afraid to open it. If Supportive Partner is present he or she can tell at once what has occurred, and will wisely leave you alone. When you finally pluck up the courage to open the envelope and read the attached sheet, whether it is a duplicated standard rejection slip (SRS) or a personal letter, you may then find, as I do, that you pass through several identifiable stages:

1 Outrage: How dare they treat me like this? Who on earth do they think they are anyway? Are they really so stupid as to be unable to see the obvious merits of this, the best novel/play/story I have ever written? Or have they got it in for me because I sent that other piece to someone else two years ago? Either they're operating a closed shop, or their reader is some smart alec straight from university who hasn't the wits to recognize a bold, original piece of work when it's staring them in the face. Or maybe it's *my* face that doesn't fit (a twinge of doubt here); maybe even . . . it couldn't be, could it, that the piece isn't quite as good as I thought it was?

2 Gloom: They're right. It's awful. I'm hopeless. What on earth was I thinking of? I wouldn't accept this rubbish from a beginner on one of my courses. I just can't cut it any more, let's face it. I'd better phone up about that job I saw adver-tised for trainee driving instructors: 'age less important than common sense and a clean licence'. I've clearly no future as a writer.

3 Rethinking: (A few hours have passed, and SP has been even more supportive than usual.) Hold on a minute, let's

calm down. The world hasn't ended, has it? There are other places I haven't tried. All right, I'll look at their letter again. What harm can it do? It's not exactly a nasty letter, after all. I mean, they are trying to explain their reservations. They know I'm not a complete idiot, or they wouldn't have bothered to say any of this, would they? Perhaps they do have a point, or two. . . .

4 Look, this isn't such a disaster. There is room for improvement, even if it does mean a lot of rewriting. All right, I'll tackle it. I'll show them; when I send it back they'll see it's the best piece of work they've had in months. If they don't, I'll try someone else. In fact I'll try someone else anyway. . . .

You simply *must* pick yourself up like this, and re-enter the fray. If you cannot do it, you will not survive as a writer. Take a few deep breaths and remember that in terms of the population as a whole, very few people have the ability to do what you do; that is, to write books, plays, stories, or anything else. Accept that you cannot please everyone, that there will be set-backs along the way, and remember that you can and will get over them.

Different writers react differently to rejection. One friend compares it to a minor bereavement; she is at first numbed by it, then it starts to hurt, then, slowly, the pain begins to subside as she gets over it and distances herself. Another writer speaks of feeling punch-drunk after a period of seemingly non-stop rejections, to the point where he expects the worst and would hardly recognize an acceptance if and when it arrived.

Survival tactics vary, and writers have naturally evolved their own means of coping. Some rant and rave, then go for a long walk or an exhausting swim; others may console themselves with drink (which can only bring temporary relief), or indulge in a grumbling session (one writer I know swears that a good moan to friends always helps him). Sooner or later, however, you must sit down and analyse the response, and try to discover what has gone wrong.

There are no easy remedies, but I would make a few suggestions which might help. Firstly, if you are working hard on a piece of work, and an envelope arrives which you believe contains a rejection, do not open it first thing. Leave it in another room and try to concentrate on your work. Open it after you have finished writing for the day, perhaps with a stiff drink to hand. Secondly, take whatever comforts you can: SP's shoulder to cry on, or the dog's, or a sympathetic friend at the other end of the phone. Remember, hundreds of writers are feeling the way you do on this very day. We all go through it, and licking one's wounds is an understandable reaction, perhaps a necessary one.

You should take each rejection individually and see what action is possible. If the respondent's letter is the slightest bit encouraging, then take heart from it. They can see you have talent, even if they can't publish or commission you on this occasion. If they suggest improvements and ask to see the revised work it is very positive – an opportunity. If they do not want this piece of work but invite you to send in something else in the future, that is also positive. But there are occasions when the response is wholly negative, and you must regroup before planning a new line of assault. Indeed, sometimes in life, attack is the best form of defence. One course of action, though it requires a degree of recklessness to implement, is to refuse to take 'No' for an answer:

The Adjustable Counter-rejection Letter

Dear____

Thank you for your letter of ____ and for the return of my manuscript/play/story/proposal.* While I understand your position I must point out, with respect, that your comments were ill-judged/inappropriate/unacceptable/utterly stupid/ lacking in even the most elementary level of professional insight.* I am therefore returning the piece herewith in order to allow you to make a more careful appraisal. I regret that I will be unable to afford you this opportunity a second time. Looking forward to your revised comments, I remain

Yours sincerely

* indicates delete as appropriate.

Trust me when I say that I am not being entirely flippant. Writers are always vulnerable, and often only too willing to accept the verdict of those who have the power to close the door in their faces. They allow themselves to be the victims; hence they can legitimately indulge in bouts of self-pity. Of course, you would be extremely unwise to send in a letter worded like this one, but you may find it therapeutic to sit down and pen your own counter-rejection blast, giving free rein to your anger. Do not, of course, post it; file it away and look at it another time, when you feel calmer.

If, on occasions, writers took a firmer line, they might be surprised to find that it can sometimes work; some people admire a hustler. Rarely, however, will someone who has rejected your work be prepared to enter into any correspondence about it; they simply do not have the time. And a standard rejection letter (usually discernible from its wording, and the way in which your name has been inserted via a template) will, of course, be no help whatsoever in assessing the reasons why the piece has been rejected. It is policy among many agencies, publishers, etc. not to give reasons, nor to reply to follow-up letters from forlorn scribes. Unfortunately, we need them more than they need us, most of the time. There are a lot of hungry writers out there.

Nevertheless, refusing to give up is essential, as proved by a friend of mine who passed her driving test on the fourteenth attempt. Persistence pays off, just as it did for John Osborne, and all those other writers who kept, and still keep, sending out their material until somebody recognizes its worth.

Lengthy, sustained periods of rejection are of course the most difficult to deal with. Even established writers sometimes endure years of this; times when they cannot seem to make any headway whatsoever. There may be any number of reasons for it. It is possible that they have become stale and are reworking or recycling old ideas, or that they are simply not producing to their best standard. It is also possible that they have failed to recognize that the market has changed, and the kind of work they have been producing is no longer wanted. Some have unrealistic expectations about the sort of work that can be commissioned in today's very competitive

106

business climate. Plays requiring fourteen actors are not likely to receive serious consideration from anyone in the theatre nowadays, or even in radio. In a very few cases, writers have acquired a reputation for being difficult in one way or another, and nobody wants to deal with them. Indeed, the difficult writer is another familiar figure, who is sometimes the last person to become aware of their situation. You will, of course, do your utmost to ensure that you do not become one of them. If you receive a disappointing phone call, for example, you must grit your teeth, remain polite, ask for time to consider what they have said, and *then* put the phone down and kick the door, or the cat, or whatever else is closest to hand.

Financially, of course, this is likely to be a difficult time for you, and hopefully the methods you have adopted *vis-à-vis* another income, as discussed in Chapter 1, will cushion you. You cannot rely on writing to sustain you, even after a modest success or two: the money earned is unlikely to be very much and, spread over a lengthy period, it will soon evaporate. A policy meeting with SP might be in order, in which the situation can be reviewed. Is it time to think about an additional source of income? Part-time work has been looked at, but remember that there are other options. You may for example let a room or rooms in your house (to someone who is quiet, of course). If you are committed to keeping up your writing, you must not allow yourself to fall at the first hurdle, or retire after the first race. There will be other races, and other seasons.

On a sober note, sometimes persistent rejection – particularly when different editors, agents, or publishers are making similar comments about your work – should sound warning bells, and encourage you to have a serious think about what you are doing. All of us at some time or other, have asked ourselves the terrible question: am I really good enough?

On a writing course about twenty years ago I met a man in his early sixties who had written twelve radio plays, each one of which had been rejected outright by the BBC; he was now working on number thirteen. Cheerful and knowledgeable (he had read every book on writing, been on every course), he still had hopes that this play would be the one. One evening a few weeks later, he failed to show up – he had died.

I tell this sad tale, not wishing to depress anyone, but to point out that while persistence, courage and self-belief are admirable and desirable qualities for writers, the ability to fool yourself is not. Competition is fierce, and the number of opportunities is limited. While I still believe firmly that talent will out, eventually, the writer who is not honest with himself or herself is going to come unstuck. One can never know whether that man's thirteenth radio play would have been accepted; I suspect it would not. Maybe there are some people who should pause, face facts and know when to quit – or at least do something else, if only for a while. But I am working on the assumption here, that you are not one of them.

If and when you achieve your first success, however, your problems are far from over.

The One-shot Writer

In the music charts of the 1960s, there were a sizeable number of bands who shone briefly in the limelight before fizzling out, never to be heard of again – the one-hit wonders. Of course, they disappeared for various reasons, sometimes things outside their control, but I cannot help thinking that those who consistently produced hit records and survived the decade were generally the most talented, as well as the most professional.

It is a fact that a lot of people are quite capable of writing a book or a play; some can even manage to pull it off twice. I have known a number who had one piece of work professionally produced before running out of steam. They are of course, long forgotten. To write consistently to a decent standard, one has to be a *writer*. Those who find themselves in the position of having had a modest success must remember that getting a foot in the door is not everything; you still have to follow up your published work with one of an equally high quality, and ideally something even better. A good agent may take steps to help a new writer over this tricky period. For example, publishers increasingly do two-book deals, or three-book deals with writers nowadays, whereby not only is your novel being published, you also have an advance to live on while you write the next one. This is a pleasant position to be in, and should allow you to take the time to work to your very best standard. Those, however, who have had one work published (by which, as always, I also mean broadcast or performed) and seem unable to make any further progress at all, must take a hard look at what they are doing. You might, for example, take a break from writing and come back to it refreshed. You might try to get some feedback from fellow-writers, publishers, agents, script editors – any professional person – as to whether you are going about things in the right way. You may even decide to try diversifying into other areas of writing, as discussed in Chapter 4.

Whatever you do, you cannot give up easily; you are finding out how tough this business is. These are your struggling years, which the majority of writers go through before making headway. Writers are craftspeople who must serve their apprenticeship and go through various rites of passage, and there will be low times along the way as well as high. If you are experiencing failure and know other writers in the same position, you can get together with them for drinks and commiseration, provided that this does not deteriorate into a regular series of depressing binges.

If you feel that you are getting nowhere and growing old, remember that most of us have felt this at some point in our lives and that failure, for a writer, is often a transient state. A footballer who hasn't made the grade by the time he is twenty-five years old is deemed a failure. But before dismissing football as a special case, we might add that a lawyer or an accountant who has not risen to a position of some status by their mid-thirties would be similarly regarded. Writers do not have retirement ages imposed upon them. Despite the sometimes depressing profusion of young writers' festivals, bursaries and competitions for the under-thirties one might do well to reflect that many writers do not get published until later, sometimes much later. Raymond Chandler was in his fifties before his famous private eye novels began to appear; Samuel Beckett did not become internationally well known until he was nearly fifty. Older people at writers' circles the length and breadth of the

109

country point to the example of Mary Wesley CBE, who was first published when she was over seventy. It could be said, however, that in this respect Ms Wesley is the exception; most writers, in my experience, begin writing in their late twenties or early thirties, and start to establish themselves in their thirties or forties.

There is a straightforward reason for this: to write successfully you need to have lived a little, and to have something to say about it. At twenty or even twenty-five you have simply not spent enough time in the world to acquire very much in the way of raw material through knowledge and life experience. Writers who are well-known exceptions, have been people of rare genius. Marlowe, who left a legacy of half a dozen major plays behind him including *Tamburlaine, Edward II* and *Doctor Faustus*, was dead at twenty-nine. Georg Büchner lived an exciting and eventful life, wrote two classic plays which are still performed, and died at twenty-three, while the poet Thomas Chatterton gave up the struggle and poisoned himself at the age of seventeen. Given the remarkable promise he had shown, one cannot help but feel that he was being somewhat hasty.

Most of us do not have the chance to live the action-packed lives of the great poets. But to write fiction of any sort one draws (sometimes unwittingly) on experience of one kind or another, even if it is second-hand. Hence, to allow the well to fill up, you need to have lived a little before you begin to write; for example, to have had relationships with people other than your parents and siblings, or to have travelled, or had a job or two, or even to have suffered a trauma of some kind. I was once sent a film script for comment, which had been written by an 18-year-old at a sixth form college. While the writing was lively and showed promise, the script itself was weak and unwieldy, and could never have worked as a film. Not only did it show all the hallmarks of the very inexperienced writer, it was even set in a sixth form college. The young writer was writing about what she knew – and all she knew about, so far, were her school and her school-friends, none of whom led very interesting lives. I would have liked to see her tackle the same subject matter ten years on, looking back from the vantage point of experience.

You need not rush into writing. It is far better to take your time; there are no penalties for late starting. A really good piece of work has never been turned down by anyone simply because the writer was middle-aged or older. It takes time to find your way (as well as your voice), and there are no maps. No writer in history has been able to predict with any degree of accuracy how their career would develop, which is far less true of those in many other walks of life, from mechanics to barristers. There are, on the whole, recognized career paths for such people; writers make their own paths.

How to Avoid Becoming a Forgotten Writer

The phenomenon of being 'famous for fifteen minutes' is now very well known, and since Andy Warhol's oft-quoted remark, countless people, from academics to embezzlers, from soldiers to streakers, have enjoyed a brief flurry of, if not success, then at least notoriety. A few of them have been able to capitalize on it, or at least to retain a healthy perspective on it and move on; the majority, of course, are now forgotten. There are, sadly, a large number of writers who fall into that category, particularly in television, which has a propensity for snapping up people with talent, working them hard and then dropping them abruptly. The Authors Licensing & Collecting Society, which exists to collect royalties for writers, regularly asks members to let them know the whereabouts of people who are owed money, and who seem to have disappeared from the map. Some turn out to be deceased, others have emigrated, but almost all are forgotten – even by their fellow-writers. While there are those (not many, I suspect) who are, for whatever reason, content to have stopped writing, there are others who become increasingly frustrated at being out in the wilderness, and worry about getting back in. This can be very difficult, and may call for unorthodox, if not desperate measures: I admire Bette Davis who, finding that film offers were not forthcoming at one point in her career, advertised in *Variety* for work. Her shameless pragmatism brought results, and the phone was soon ringing again.

Let us assume by now that you have had your first piece of luck, that your work has been seen in print, or perhaps heard over the airwaves. You might even call yourself a professional, even if you are flat broke. This is in fact a dangerous time in your career, for you are not yet (I assume) well known outside your own small circle. You may have reached a plateau, and need to consolidate your reputation before climbing further. If you have an agent by now, they may be able to help, having had many writers pass through the stage at which you now find yourself. They might advise you to put yourself about, to attend important functions and gatherings, and mix with influential people (networking again), the thought of which may fill you with horror. If it does, they should be sensitive enough to understand this and to take on much of the responsibility for pushing you forward by arranging meetings with publishers and producers, for example, or suggesting you for projects – in short, selling you. Agents are in fact losing money while they do this; they see it as an investment, bringing forward a writer whom they feel confident will do well in the future.

If you have no agent, this might be the time to try and get one, when you can point to some measure of success, which shows that you have already made a start. Select some suitable names from a writers' handbook and write them a polite letter, enclosing a smart c.v. and evidence of your published work (if you have some favourable reviews, these are excellent). With luck, someone might be willing to take you on, provided you sound as if you know where you are going next. They will be less enthusiastic if you seem too bedazzled by your modest success. When dealing with professionals, you must try to sound professional even if you don't feel it. This means showing that you are committed to your work, and have the will and the talent to move forward.

If you cannot get an agent, or if you decide not to bother trying for the present, you must then take pains to maintain and build on the contacts you have made. This means keeping in touch. An occasional letter or phone call telling people what you are working on can keep your name afloat, but do not do it too often. You must try to discern, from their tone of voice, or the wording of written replies, whether they are happy to hear from you, or whether you are outstaying your welcome. As soon as you have a new piece written you will, of course, send it to the individual editor or producer you worked with the first time, but make sure first that they have not moved on. Authors often complain that no sooner have they established a good working relationship with some editor, than they change jobs. You need to try, if possible, to keep your ear to the ground in your own field, which means reading relevant publications to see what is happening. The theatre world, for example, is surprisingly small; humble assistant directors one knew ten years ago can suddenly emerge in positions of authority, with the power to commission writers, or at least to point you towards others who can.

It is also vitally important to make new contacts whenever possible. A brief letter with a c.v. to a new agency, or publication, or theatre group, or production company that is starting up, may result in an invitation to come in for a chat. Announcements and advertisements in arts newsletters are useful, and your local regional arts board probably produces their own; if you contact them they will put you on the mailing list free of charge. Word of mouth contacts are also important, and are sometimes the most valuable of all: 'I was talking with so-and-so last week and they suggested I get in touch with you about my new project . . .' Name-dropping is perfectly acceptable when you are a writer hungry for work.

It should be clear by now that in today's climate writers must take more responsibility than ever for furthering their own careers. The world will not come to you, and, like it or not, this is a business. While many of us are very bad business people, we could still make a little time to write letters, to keep connections alive and to find out what is going on. We are, after all, professionals.

Remember that rejection is not in itself a mark of failure. It happens to the best of us, and it happens for many reasons. It does not mean that you cannot write.

Remember too, that failure is simply a state of mind; anyone can feel like a failure at some point in their lives. Among the rich and famous there are those who still secretly regard themselves as failures; who sold out at some stage in their career, or failed to start the family they longed for; who never realized their full potential, or their true ambitions. Look how some have ended up: by what yardstick other than enormous wealth would one judge Howard Hughes a success?

If you have talent, if you commit yourself to pursuing it and refuse to be knocked off course by the icebergs of indifference, rejection, or hard criticism, if, as Lady Macbeth urged, you '. . . screw your courage to the sticking-place . . .', you will not fail. Even if you think you have failed for a time, there is a simple answer: why not try writing about it? You may yet strike gold.

8

Coping with Success

Martin Amis' novel *The Information* contains a very entertaining account of two writers who are turning forty. Richard is struggling, impecunious, unrecognized, and exhibits many of the hallmarks of failure. His friend (and rival) Gwyn is, by contrast, successful with a capital S, confident, sought after, sickeningly rich, surrounded by technical gadgetry and other celebrity trappings. Perhaps they represent the two sides of one writer's personality. Is success for a writer to do only with wealth and fame? In ages past great artists often died in poverty and obscurity, but the fact that nobody recognized their worth while they were alive did not prevent them from being great artists. Posterity is also subjective; reappraisal reveals a genius where there was once a nobody. In one way, then, the artist or writer did succeed; they were simply unable to capitalize on it.

Becoming an established writer brings its own problems. For one thing, people will now have high expectations of you. There is pressure to produce work of an ever-higher standard. Distractions soon multiply; more people want to talk to you, to claim acquaintance with you, to share in your success, however modest. There exists the hope that some of it may rub off on them, or that now you are moving up in the world you might be able to steer them in more promising directions. Success, said Edmund Burke (if rather pompously), is 'the only infallible criterion of wisdom to vulgar minds'.

Success may come in various forms and, like the devil in some medieval morality play, it may not be recognizable on first appearance. A book which is accepted for publication and earns you a modest four-figure advance may exceed all expectations in terms of sales figures and be reprinted. It could cross the Atlantic, be translated into other languages and end up being made into a film, conceivably making you a millionaire (such things have happened). A play which begins life in some provincial theatre, earning you perhaps £4,000, might travel to the West End of London and thence to Broadway, with spectacular results.

For most writers, however, success means a long haul, a slow progression from obscurity to becoming a recognized name. You cross several Rubicons: that first professional publication or production, then the struggle to repeat the process, then with luck and application another one, and slowly, often imperceptibly, things begin to change. Competitions you see advertised in magazines include the proviso that entry is restricted to writers with not more than one work (or two, or three) professionally produced. You are deemed to be past such things now. People ask you who your agent is, assuming that you must have one. Others make the alarming assumption that you must earn a lot of money, and reactions to you vary from admiration to envy and, at times, bitterness. Still others accost Supportive Partner and ask him or her in hushed tones what it's like living with a celebrity. The novelist John Fowles was washing his car one day when two tourists appeared at the gate. Finally one plucked up the courage to ask: 'Tell me, what's it like working for such a famous writer?' They had assumed he was the chauffeur.

In fact, few writers achieve celebrity status, and apart from popular novelists many of them are not well-known names outside of the literary world, or the theatre, or film world (how many people can name the screen-writers of *Titanic*, or *Saving Private Ryan*, or the scriptwriters of *Coronation Street*?) Furthermore, as we have seen from the start of this book, surprisingly few writers make more than what might be called an average income. The first topic we might consider in relation to success, therefore, is that of money.

Contracts

It is rather exciting to be faced, for the first time in your career, with a professional contract to sign. It can also be a little daunting, with all those clauses and unfamiliar terms, not to mention the fee being offered. How do you know what is normal, and what is not? Are they expecting you to take it or leave it, or to negotiate?

If you are new to all this, do not yet have an agent and feel you are on dangerous ground, you need help. This might be a good time to join one of the writers' organizations, the Writers' Guild, or the Society of Authors. Receipt of your first professional contract entitles you to membership and therefore some advice. Needless to say, you will not rush into signing anything without getting it thoroughly checked over. You will also be told the current scales of fees, and what you might reasonably expect for a particular piece of work. Even the BBC, which has standard contracts, can be flexible when it comes to fees. There are fixed rates in, say, radio drama, which rise depending on whether you already have broadcast work to your credit. A first-timer, naturally enough, is on the lowest rate, and does not have much in the way of bargaining power. Established writers, on the other hand, seldom settle for the sum they are entitled to, and their agents can often 'talk up' the figure, if only slightly. There is a tacit acceptance in the industry that professionals are entitled to the occasional perk; for example, radio writers who have had over two hours of drama broadcast on the network are not only on the 'established' rate, they also receive travel expenses and a daily attendance fee for being at recordings, a recognition that they are taking time away from their writing while they are at the studio. However, such benefits have come under closer scrutiny in the cost-conscious climate of recent years and may not last for ever. It is no longer an easy ride – if it ever was.

Contracts vary enormously. If you are dealing directly with a publisher, one hopes that they are signatories to the Minimum Terms Agreement (not all of them are), a copy of which is available from the Writers' Guild or the Society of Authors. This sets out the terms and conditions to be observed in all contracts between publishers and authors, in respect of such matters as copyright, royalties, warranty and indemnity, etc., etc. If the publisher is not a signatory to the MTA they will issue their own contract, which should be examined carefully. If you are in doubt about anything you can legitimately ask them to clarify it. It is possible that you can get an agent to negotiate for you, if only on a one-off basis. They will, of course, demand their usual percentage, but it may be well worth it; they do this sort of thing all the time and know the territory, the jargon and the legal pitfalls. If you cannot or do not wish to seek help from an agent, or one of the writers' organizations, you can, of course, take your contract along to a solicitor for advice. Bear in mind, however, that as a very new writer you are unlikely to be able to demand very much in the way of changes to the agreement, and it may well be a case of take it or leave it. Of course, you feel vulnerable at this stage, and perhaps afraid of losing out altogether if you appear difficult. Nevertheless, you must be polite but firm, and only sign when you have got the best deal you think you can get. As things progress you will learn how the business operates, and next time you will be better prepared. The higher you climb, in fact, the more complex contracts can become (and the more negotiable the fees). In certain areas which involve potentially large sums of money (and also higher risks) like film and West End theatre, the contracts are very lengthy and elaborate, going into details that might at first amaze you, such as T-shirt rights and other spin-offs. In these cases you will almost certainly deal via an agent; indeed, you would be unwise not to.

Usually contracts or agreements are sent in duplicate, with a space at the end for your signature as well as that of the other party. You sign and return one copy, and keep the other (make sure that they have signed it). If there is just one copy you will of course make a photocopy of it for your own records.

A contract is not the end of the story, it is a beginning. As matters progress you will need to refer to the paper you have signed from time to time, because things happen at various stages (half on signature, half on delivery of work is a common enough rule of thumb). In the fields of, say, television and film there are more payment stages than in radio; for example, in film, phrases like '£0,000 to be paid on first day of principal photography' appear. Usually, writers are paid a portion of their fee in advance, a portion when the first draft of a script is delivered, perhaps another when the final draft is ready and another on transmission or release. Then follow other fees (royalties and residuals) for things like repeats, overseas sales, educational broadcasts and so on. It can get complicated. It also means that a piece of work may earn you money years after it first appeared. Nowadays, with cable, satellite broadcasting and the Internet things are even more complex, and hence writers are more vulnerable than ever. Copyright is being eroded in certain areas which are difficult to police. We writers have tried to safeguard ourselves, through time-consuming and often difficult negotiation, by hammering out agreements with the various controlling bodies. But not everyone signs up to these (or even adheres to them), and at bottom the writer often feels alone, at the mercy of powerful companies and organizations which exploit 'the talent', as writers and performers are collectively known. There are, regrettably, still grounds for such fears.

Commissions and Advances

A commission means quite simply that your work is being bought (like placing an order for a suit, you being the tailor). A contract, and then (one hopes) an initial sum of money, like a deposit, will follow. Use of these two terms varies somewhat: a play that is already written, and is then taken up by radio, or the theatre is still spoken of as being commissioned; however, when professional writers talk about a commission, they usually mean that they have been contracted to write a particular work.

New writers are hardly ever commissioned because, as mentioned earlier, even if you have a great idea for a series, nobody knows whether you are capable of writing the scripts – let alone to a good enough standard – and delivering them on time. You have to show evidence of a track record, by which time you will in any case be known to individual producers, editors and the like, who might approach you. It is very gratifying to receive a letter from a producer whom you have never met, saying something like: 'I liked your piece *Sleepless in Solihull* enormously, and wonder if you would be interested in working with me on a new project . . .'. If you are sensible, you will express interest even if you are too busy

119

already; here is a potentially useful contact for the future. (Stringing them along, however, will do you no good at all.)

A commission means that, after signing the contract or agreement, you are normally paid an advance sum, which in theory you are supposed to live on while you write the piece of work. In reality such advances (also known by other names such as first-half fees, or first-part instalments) are seldom large enough to last long. With a radio play, depending on its length, the first-half fee is unlikely to be more than about £1,500, perhaps less. With, say, a television series it will be considerably more, but the amount of work involved is probably much greater. In the theatre rates vary depending on various factors, such as which professional body the theatre, or theatre company belongs to (and hence which scale of fees they employ). However prestigious they are, you are unlikely to receive more than a very few thousand pounds before production. If a play does well further royalties should follow, usually as a percentage of the box-office returns. Publishers' advances for books probably show the widest variation; they can range from a paltry three-figure advance to the sort of lottery-sized figures one reads about for best-selling novelists.

Many writers, if they can, take on more than one commission at once, without necessarily letting either party know that theirs is not the only piece of work in progress. This way of working may seem daunting to you at first, but it can be beneficial; for example, when you are sick of the sight of one project, you might put it aside for a while and work on the other one. Of course, there are drawbacks, like the producer or editor phoning you for a progress report on their project while you are totally immersed in the other one. Some quick thinking is called for, and perhaps a little bluffing. I keep a sort of progress sheet above the desk reminding me of what stage I am at with the other piece. Even so, I have been thrown into panic by a busy producer phoning on a Monday morning and starting the conversation with something like:

'Look, that speech in scene seventeen we were talking about the other day – it just won't work. Can you fax me some cuts by eleven o'clock?'

But I have no right to grumble; I am lucky to be busy.

*

To be a commissioned writer is a good feeling, and even if your income is still dependent largely on Supportive Partner, the part-time job, the lodger, or the dwindling savings, you have earned the right to be treated as a professional. The people who have commissioned you will treat you as such in any case; since they are at work at ten o'clock in the morning, they probably expect you to be at your desk too (hence an answering machine becomes an important piece of equipment).

At this point in your career it is wise to make sure you are well organized. Your working environment, which you no doubt created some time ago on the advice given in Chapter 2 is more important than ever now; not only is there work in progress, but the paper work and correspondence are probably multiplying at an alarming rate. If you have not arranged some sort of filing system already, you should do so now. If you use a computer, most of your work will be on disc and hence will require very little space, though some proper storage boxes, clearly labelled, are a necessary investment. But correspondence will arrive by post anyway, and you need a filing cabinet or at least some strong box files to keep everything in order (I find lever arch files useful for things like correspondence). Completed work I keep in the filing cabinet in hanging files labelled in red ink for published or produced pieces, black for everything else. I also have a 'dead file' (a bulging shoe-box) into which I shove everything that falls by the wayside. Among its contents are projects that barely got started, others which were rejected and others still that were well developed and almost commissioned. Whatever the reason for their demise, I do not throw them away: ideas can and have been reused, perhaps in a different form, sometimes many years later. I think of them as a kind of reserve stock.

Now that you are getting used to being a working writer and have had a taste of success, you need to be aware of the temptations that may follow. The first of these is the tendency to feel euphoric, that it is really happening at last, and that there is no stopping you now.

Keeping Both Feet on the Ground

In Arthur Miller's beautifully written, if somewhat guarded autobiography *Timebends: A Life*, he describes his state of mind just after the early success of his famous play *Death of a Salesman*. He found himself in the position of not having to go to work, of being able to spend his time anyway he chose, of being able to write what he wanted – or not write at all. He began to take long walks, to look about him a great deal, to observe people who hadn't the time to do what he was doing. Of course he was a fine writer on the threshold of a glittering career, but in 1949 he did not know that; he felt very lucky, and rather guilty.

Self-discipline is important at the first stage of your professional writing career. Many of us have felt like basking in our success for a while, phoning up friends and arranging to meet, as if we wish to prolong the euphoria for as long as possible. We might be tempted to treat ourselves, having banked that first cheque, to some new clothes, or a weekend away. That is fine, so long as you remember that all of this is, simply, irrelevant; it will not help you move forward with your work. Sooner or later you must, simply go to the desk and start the next thing. The fact that your book may be selling well, or your play touring to packed audiences may be far less important than you think, for in a month's time, or three months, or a year, it might be all over, the work fading in the public mind and the money disappearing. Even established novelists with half a dozen books published can find their earnings dwindling, and must put their agents under pressure to secure the next deal, and the next. Playwrights too are hunting for commissions, which are fairly scarce nowadays. There are no guarantees (feast-or-famine again), and it is down to you to build on your success and continue to do your best work – again and again.

If you have developed a good working routine by now (which ideally you will have), make every effort to keep to it, even if your circumstances are changing. If mornings are for writing then leave the mail unopened and do your admin, phoning and bill-paying later. Nothing should be allowed to side-track you from making progress with your next piece of work. If you are finding it difficult to concentrate, there are remedies. Writer friends suggest the following – we have heard of some before, but they are worth recounting here:

1 Get up earlier – even if you have to force yourself – and go straight to the desk with just a cup of tea or coffee, or a glass of fruit juice. Write for an hour at least; then you can have breakfast, wave the children off to school, or whatever. Supportive Partner will need to be aware of any new routine and to adjust to it, which may mean some negotiation is called for. When you go back to work later (not too much later) you should be able to pick up again.

2 Keep distractions down, even more firmly than before. Put the answering machine on when writing and return any calls later. Do not answer the door, even to well-wishers bearing champagne. It is better to invite them for a meal one evening, and celebrate with them then. You need not feel guilty if you have done a day's writing.

3 Do everyday things when you have finished writing. You are not a film star. Unlike film stars, writers do their own shopping, cleaning and cooking, mow their own lawns, paint their own ceilings. Writers are artisans who operate in a cottage industry. We do not have an army of personal managers, therapists, style consultants and make-up experts to pick us up after a night's debauchery, perform miracles on us and send us on to the set, and there is a limit to how many of these functions SP can perform at any one time. We have to be, in the jargon of the sales industry, self-starters. Nobody can write for you. You have to produce the goods, again and again.

4 Try to make family life as normal as possible, as our Prime Minister says he does. Spend time with the family if you have one, or with parents, or friends who do not treat you differently now that you are a writer. If they are honest they will put the brake on and stop you from becoming too giddy with success, or from boring people to death by talking constantly about your work.

If you keep your feet on the ground, in time you should be able to adjust to your new status. If you are dealing regularly with professionals (agents, editors, publishers, producers) who may, for example, be asking when your next piece will be ready, you will find that this helps you to keep a sense of proportion. They are at their work, and so are you. In fact, the dangers that lurk unseen in the months and years ahead may be ones you had at one time never expected to face at all.

Criticism and How to Handle It

Noel Coward telephoned a critic who had given one of his plays a particularly hostile review: 'I am sitting in the smallest room in the house,' the Master said, 'with your review in front of me. Shortly it will be behind me.'

Like rejection, criticism goes with the territory for writers, as it does for all those in the arts. If you put any piece of work out into the public domain people have a right to say what they think of it, and you must accept that not everyone will like it; some may loathe it. Eavesdropping in the foyer during the interval or after a performance of their work, is something most playwrights have done at one time or another, and such experiences can range from the delightful to the deeply depressing. Reactions to criticism of arts practitioners themselves, range from the virulent: 'All critics should be assassinated' (Man Ray), to the tolerant, or even complimentary: 'Great critics build a home for truth' (Raymond Chandler). For a dialogue about the value of artistic criticism, Oscar Wilde's 'The Critic as Artist' is worth reading, if only for its wit.

I am unlikely to forget the experience of getting my very first bad review. Without going into details, I can say that for a while it made me feel very small, very foolish and a very bad writer. It was so unpleasant that the publicity officer of the company that was performing the play could not find a single positive phrase to lift from it; it had been carefully crafted to be useless on that score and, it seemed, to cause maximum hurt to the writer. Why? I asked myself a dozen times, as I reread it again and again in mounting disbelief. I had never met the reviewer, or even heard of him, and he presumably knew nothing of me, so why was he so hostile? What had I done to provoke such scorn, such sarcasm?

Later, when I had recovered a little and been comforted by others, I began to realize that the critic had his own agenda. He was young, perhaps a hungry writer himself, trying to make a reputation in a competitive business (he worked for a well-known London publication). One does not make a reputation by writing lukewarm reviews, or even positive ones. Critics are expected to wield the knife on occasions, and to wield it eloquently. There are, after all, published anthologies of witty critiques on the shelves of libraries, and some writers have even been happy to play gamekeeper and poacher at the same time, George Bernard Shaw being an obvious example.

My play, the critic clearly disliked, but what upset me was the way in which he chose to express it; for example, by quoting lines out of context to make them sound ludicrous. When I was told later by the theatre staff that he had never given any production under their roof a good review, I began to feel better – and to feel angry. Now I understood the rage authors feel, when the work they have sweated and strained over is lambasted in print by someone who knows nothing of it, who hasn't even paid for the book or the theatre ticket and who will be busy lambasting some other hapless scribe tomorrow, with your name already a fading memory. As time went on, I learned more. A critic from one national daily paper was ordered by his arts editor to cover my play instead of going up to the West End. Furious at being made to sit in a small fringe theatre and review work that he considered somehow beneath him, he produced a scathing review. This, combined with the poisonous, earlier review, killed off the play's chances in the first few days and resulted in a near-empty theatre for the rest of the four-week run: a clear demonstration of the power that critics can wield. In New York it is much worse. A well-known critic like Clive Barnes, whom every theatre-goer reads, can kill a play or a musical stone-dead after the opening night, resulting in possible bankruptcies and for all I know, suicides. Such is show business. An interesting statistic at time of writing is that in the dozen years from 1987 to 1999, 399 shows have opened on Broadway, of which all but 28 closed, many after very short runs indeed.

Before arousing your suspicions that perhaps my play really was bad and that I was simply refusing to face facts, let me add that the reviews elsewhere were almost consistently favourable during the play's long tour, before and after its London run. By those people who made up the tiny London audiences, it was also well received. The London critics, it seemed, had their own fish to fry, and I was in the pan that particular week.

There are a number of schools of thought when it comes to criticism. Some writers, like some actors, say they never read reviews; others admit that they have learned from them. A well-informed critic of real insight (they do exist) is usually a competent writer too, and can add a great deal to one's appreciation and understanding of a piece of work (Michael Billington is a well-respected example). For the writer, to read a glowing review is, of course, a very pleasant experience, but more than simply appealing to one's vanity it should encourage you and inform you about the strengths of your work. If we could all read unfavourable reviews in the same light, we might learn a lot about our weaknesses and resolve to try and do better, but unfortunately it is not so simple as that. In the end it comes down to whether or not one can trust the reviewer. A critique is, after all, merely one person's subjective opinion. Some, as I have illustrated, I would never trust; they may have reasons for bashing your book or play that have little to do with its quality. Traditionally, critics were seen as failed writers turning a quick penny, in Shelley's words: 'As a bankrupt thief turns thief-taker, so an unsuccessful author turns critic'. Nowadays that may be less true, indeed established writers often find themselves in demand to review the work of others, which at times can be a difficult task: what to do, if the latest novel by a writer whom you think of as a friend falls into your hands, and you consider it an unmitigated disaster?

We have to take the criticism, as we do all of life's brickbats. To take it to heart, however, is dangerous; your confidence can be damaged, and this will affect your writing. At such low moments, get out a piece of work which you are pleased with and reread it to remind yourself how well you can write. Then make a big effort to get on with the work in hand. If you did it once, you can do it again.

Despite Noel Coward's example, most writers will say that they never enter into correspondence with a critic (normally the critic would not respond in any case). My advice is to file the bad reviews away and forget about them; the good ones you should use whenever and wherever possible. You can photocopy them and paste them up into a publicity sheet, or simply edit them and send them out with samples of your work, showing what a success you are. Modesty is not a quality that is highly valued in the worlds of publishing, broadcasting or theatre. However, it is possible to come unstuck. One agent, who had read my script accompanied by the selection of glorious reviews, sent me a letter which reads: 'I am sorry that we do not feel sufficiently committed to the play to offer representation. I realize this flies in the face of the fine reviews your work has had, and therefore we're clearly not the right agency for you.' On some occasions one must admit defeat, gird the loins and move on.

Spreading Yourself too Thinly

One of the common pitfalls for writers who begin to find themselves in demand, after any initial period of euphoria has passed, is that they try to do too much. They are so pleased to be busy that they say yes to everything. Do a second book by Christmas? Of course! Adapt another one for television? Try and stop me! Write an article for this magazine, review a couple of books for that one, give a talk to the local WI – delighted! You're on a roll now, you're a professional writer, and at last people recognize your worth.

You may, of course, enjoy doing a variety of different tasks; some people do all the things mentioned above and more, and are happy to do them. If you love putting words on paper, then you will probably find that you can turn your hand to different kinds of work in any case. If you have the talent to write a book, play, or stories, you can almost certainly write a review, an article, possibly a script, or even a survival guide. The question is, if you start doing all of these regularly, are you running the risk of becoming a jack of all trades? Rather than spread yourself too thinly, ought you not to concentrate on what you do best?

Glancing back to Chapter 3, I hope that in the course of your 'apprenticeship' years you try different sorts of writing, different forms and genres, and discover what sort of writer you really are: novelist, poet, playwright, screen-writer, biographer, or whatever. Of course, you can diversify, for all the reasons mentioned earliery – and you may have to. But once you become published and begin to achieve some measure of success, you should find out whether you are comfortable carrying on with the same sort of writing, or whether you feel a change of direction may be beneficial. If you wish to consolidate your reputation, and hopefully earn a reasonably steady income, it may be best (or even vital) to continue writing, say, the crime novels that have brought you to the attention of the reading public. Some very successful writers are in fact known for a series of books featuring one character, but for little else, like Simenon's Maigret, for example. Simenon was apparently content to be in that position; others, as Arthur Conan Doyle did with Holmes, find the continuing popularity of their famous creation to be a millstone around the neck.

The temptation to take on lots of work (I should grumble) is understandable. Nobody wants to be a flash in the pan, a one-shot writer. Now that opportunity has arrived at long last, you wish to grab it with both hands. I strongly advise, however, that you step back for a moment and take time to make sure things are going in the direction you want them to. If you have an agent now, you might want to talk it over with him or her; they know the markets, and the market trends, and they ought to be able to see your strengths and where you should best apply them. If you are enjoying writing your next book, and can even see your way to the one after that, this is a very positive sign. If the opportunity to make a sideways move presents itself (a radio or television adaptation, perhaps) and this excites you, that too sounds promising. Writers must, in the end, trust their gut feelings as to what is right for them. Once you have found what sort of work you really want to do next, you will be unhappy with anything else.

Before leaping eagerly forward, however, do bear in mind that there is another danger ahead, perhaps a surprising one: that of becoming *too prolific*.

One does not have to look too far for examples of writers who turned out work at a frightening rate, from Grub Street hacks to some of the great names. The Spanish dramatist Calderón de La Barca wrote hundreds of plays in his long life, of which more than a hundred still survive. Sophocles wrote over a hundred, of which only a handful have survived. William Shakespeare's canon of thirty-seven plays and some poetry looks modest by comparison, as does Alan Ayckbourn's output of fifty or so plays. But what really matters here, quality or quantity? At the risk of becoming snobbish, few of us would claim that the work of those pulp fiction, or romance writers, some of whom produce a book per month, or even one a fortnight, would stand comparison with the novels of Iris Murdoch or Salman Rushdie. Kingsley Amis said that he could not finish a novel in under a year, and it usually took closer to two. I have heard the playwright Christopher Hampton make similar claims: two years, he reckoned, to complete a new play. It took Joseph Heller almost a decade (well, eight years) of spare-time writing to produce *Catch 22*; I am willing to bet that he feels it was time well spent.

Some writers will say that there is a limit to how many books anyone has in them; that after a while you can easily begin repeating yourself, or recycling tired old ideas. Are you content to be known as the author of a few good books or plays, or the author of a hundred that made you a living but ended up on the remaindered shelves (i.e. unsold copies sold off cheaply by the publishers)? In the end, of course, you will make the decisions; I am sounding, once again, a cautionary note. If you find that you can write at your best, and still write quite prolifically, you are fortunate. Many fine writers in fact, can and do work quickly. Simenon, already mentioned, could turn out a new Maigret novel in fifteen days of solid writing. But hurrying to finish a new book, play, or anything else and sending it off without taking time to look it over properly and revise, may, in the long run, do you no good. The standard of your work will slip, and people will notice it quite quickly. Indeed publishers recognize this factor, and usually allow ample time for you to do your next work. Many are even surprised when you deliver the manuscript on time; they are used to writers pleading for another month, or three, or six. Being over-eager to write novel number two and see it in print may in effect prove counter-productive; the work might need to be extensively rewritten, or it might not even get published at all.

You must simply take as long as it takes, maintain your very best standard, and try not to think too much about the money. If your second book or play is even better than the first, then your reputation should begin to grow in any case, and the rewards will follow in time. It is not a disaster if your readers have to wait a little – they will appreciate the work all the more. Turning out material at a frantic rate is unwise for any writer who takes themselves seriously and cares about the quality of their writing. George Eliot expressed herself elegantly on the subject, as always, saying: 'I have the conviction that excessive literary production is a social offence'.

Of course, if you *are* naturally prolific, and do not wish to appear ubiquitous, there, is a simple answer.

Pseudonyms

Seeing your work published under a pseudonym for the first time can produce an odd mixture of feelings. On the one hand, you may be disappointed that you will not be known as the author of the work. On the other hand, you are relieved that you will not be known as the author of the work. It all depends on the work.

Pseudonyms have long been employed by writers, often for sound practical reasons. Daniel Defoe might have wished he had been able to preserve his anonymity when he found himself in the pillory for writing dissenting tracts. When he did preserve it, in *A Journal of the Plague Year*, many people believed that the book was written by someone who had really lived through the great plague of 1665; in fact Defoe was barely five years old at the time – he had merely done his research well. One may easily add that reasons why writers may wish to remain anonymous are still with us three centuries later, viz. Salman Rushdie's experiences since the publication of *The Satanic Verses*. The Brontë sisters famously sent their first novels to a publisher together under the male pseudonyms Acton, Currer and Ellis Bell (for Ann, Charlotte and Emily). Of course, the publishers were not fooled for an instant, and declared that the three books showed such similarities of style, they were clearly the work of the same man.

Charlotte, in fact, continued to be published for years under the name Currer Bell until, the secret having worn thin, she finally abandoned it. In the nineteenth century many women used men's names: it was difficult to get published otherwise. Nowadays one may have other reasons, and a pseudonym might be used not merely to remain anonymous, but to project a different persona from the one your real name suggests. When the playwright Martin Crimp won a *Time Out* story competition in 1982, he submitted his entry under the pseudonym Karen Kopinski, explaining later that he had a hunch they would prefer to give the prize to a female Pole. Some romantic novels, which the almost exclusively female readership expect to be written by women, are in fact written by men under a *nom de plume*. (Of the eight writers short-listed for the 1999 Romantic Novel of the Year one, Jessica Stirling, is a man writing under a pseudonym.) Erotic writings, not surprisingly, rarely bear the name of the real author. As we saw in Chapter 4, some established writers employ a range of names, sometimes without any special desire for anonymity; Ruth Rendell for example, some of whose books bear the phrase 'Ruth Rendell writing as Barbara Vine'. Ellis Peters is another writer who, like the Brontës, uses a writing name with the same initials as her own, Edith Pargeter. However, we would all wish to avoid the example of the American novelist Upton Sinclair, who apparently at times forgot which pseudonym he had employed for which piece of work.

When I wrote a western novel, I quickly discovered that nearly everyone writing in this field uses a pseudonym in keeping with the genre. English names are generally unsuitable (as J.T. Edson knew, many years ago); the author should sound American, rugged and very male. The name Cecil Partington is unlikely to inspire readers of westerns to buy the book; something like Clint Cordite might. Glance at the covers of a few westerns and you will begin to see that many of the names do not, somehow, ring true, not that it matters. How many fans of Jack London, Zane Grey, Max Brand or J.T. Edson care whether or not those are their real names? Not all are pseudonyms though; Zane Grey started his working life as a dentist. The point is that his name doesn't suggest he was a dentist, it suggests a writer of westerns who knows what he is about.

The writer can have fun thinking up pseudonyms, but before we become flippant let us remember that they have a real purpose and can make all the difference in selling your book. Publishers will not be impressed if you take the matter lightly, nor are they fools; a student of mine tried to use the Greek-sounding Krys Dosyllis, without success (read the surname backwards).

You do not need to use a pseudonym when you first submit a work; it can be decided upon later. There will be no shortage of offers from family and friends to help you think one up. Be clear about its purpose, and what it is intended to convey, whether it is a serious alternative writing name, or an obvious cover.

Capitalizing on Success

It seems common sense to state that when you have achieved a degree of success with your writing, you will want to make the most of it and consolidate your position. There are three main aspects to this: the personal, the financial and the professional.

The personal is, of course, the most sensitive area. As we have seen, those closest to you will have some adjusting to do, now that you (presumably) work permanently from home and live a writer's life. If Supportive Partner is at home a lot, the strain may start to show. Arguments over keeping the noise down, over who should answer the phone or the door, or when to take lunch, can grow out of all proportion until they become the last straw, like leaving the top off the proverbial tube of toothpaste. I suggest you reread Chapters 5 and 6. You need, as we have seen, to keep your feet on the ground. You may have become obsessive about your work – it is difficult for a writer to be anything else – but you are, are you not, doing what you wanted to do all along? Take a minute or two, maybe once a week, to rejoice in the fact, and think of all those who are toiling away on building sites, in factories and offices, in boardrooms and classrooms at this very moment, and wishing they were somewhere else. You are the lucky one. Enjoy your luck, and let it infuse every part of your life.

The financial dimension of your writing life has now become more important than ever. If you are self-employed you will need to keep careful records of all income and expenditure. You may decide that you can afford the services of an accountant which will probably cost you at least £100 a year, but will of course relieve you of a great deal of additional work, apart from bringing other benefits like tax advice. It is vital for you to keep in mind the fact that your earnings can and probably will vary enormously from year to year (the roller-coaster existence we looked at in the first chapter), and making some financial provision for the future while you can, may be the best decision you ever take. In America a lot of writers take out unemployment insurance. You can do the equivalent, whether it be an Individual Savings Account (ISA) or a simple savings account; your bank or building society should have staff who are there to give free financial advice. You might even want to buy into a pension plan. Writers have traditionally been improvident people, but in fact, most of the ones I know have learned to be very careful with their money, and to put some of it by for the rainy months which they know will come sooner or later. A friend who wrote for a well-known television series, earning handsome fees, now speaks of his relief that he put much of it into savings, for he has hit a bad patch and is, in effect, still living off that series which ended years ago. Keeping something back would seem to be common sense, even if your agent is speaking glowingly of a prospective West End transfer, overseas sales, or a delicious five-figure advance for the next book; even agents can get carried away on occasions, or be let down by some third party. The professional writer can be professional in all ways, including the running of his or her one-person business.

The professional aspect of your life is what we have in fact been discussing all through this chapter, if not all through this book. To summarize: as a working writer you will have ensured that you have the conditions and the environment in which to do your best work. You will not allow yourself to be distracted from the work, and you should only deal now with professional people (agents, editors, producers, publishers, etc.) who are relevant to it. Becoming even a tiny bit famous has many drawbacks, which is one reason why a lot of writers become increasingly reclusive as they get older, but as we have seen, the main disadvantage is that fame can actually stop you writing, which defeats the object. You have a career now, which should be treated in a similar way to any previous career you may have had; for example, dealing sensibly with financial matters, deciding which direction you want to take next, and how you want things to develop in the longer term. Many writers, it is true, are not among life's planners – myself included. But there are times when I wish that I had thought more deeply about what I was doing, and what I really wanted to do next. You have come this far, and no doubt it has been something of a struggle; don't lose it now.

9

Into the Sunset

Before this survival guide grew into its present form I had the idea of writing a rather different book, with the working title *The Struggling Writer*. It occurred to me that quite a lot of people fashion whole careers out of being struggling writers. Writing must be one of the few professions in which, at an age when most people are beginning to think about retiring, its practitioners are still trying to get established. Many never do, and yet as we have seen, the knowledge, supported by convincing evidence that they probably never will, seldom deters them.

I hope that by the time you have reached your twilight years, you have either established yourself in one field or another, or accepted the fact that you are unlikely to do so now. This is not defeatist talk, it is being realistic. There are few sadder spetacles than those retired teachers, bank-managers and gas engineers (to take three professions at random) who have at last got the time to write and are eager to make their mark, refusing to face the fact that they have already done so, as teachers, bank-managers or gas engineers. Hardly any of them are likely to become published writers now. Writing is a career, not a hobby, which requires, as we have seen, a commitment from the outset. If you are content, however, to treat it as a retirement hobby with no great expectations of reward, that is healthy enough and can bring you a great deal of pleasure and satisfaction; it can surely do no harm.

There is, as I have said already, no compulsory retirement age for writers. Many go on until they drop, or at least until they can no longer hold a pen, and of course, it matters not a jot how old the writer is if the work is good. We need not look far for examples of those who are still producing at a ripe old age. As I write this, Doris Lessing, in her eightieth year, has a new novel published set in the future, while across the Atlantic Arthur Miller and Saul Bellow, both in their mid-eighties, are no doubt busy at their desks. Recognition for writers often comes late in life in any case. Kingsley Amis was in his mid-sixties before winning the Booker prize for *The Old Devils*, while William Golding was seventy when he won it for *Rites of Passage*. The Nobel prize for Literature is awarded in recognition of the body of work a writer has contributed to the world; hence recipients are never young, usually in their sixties or older. To write a sizeable number of works to a high standard takes a lifetime.

In fact, writers hardly ever stop, because they either cannot, or do not want to. For many it is a *raison d'être* and proof that they are still alive and cognitive. But here is a dilemma that has to be faced: should one go on until the very last gasp if the standard of work has fallen away badly? Many people were moved some years ago by the example of the dying Dennis Potter, struggling bravely to finish his last plays for television, *Karaoke* and *Cold Lazarus*. He knew they would be his last plays, as did everyone else, and this was his final chance to make some sort of definitive, or at least parting statement. Unfortunately, neither piece is his finest and one of them was, sadly, disappointing. Working under that sort of pressure, not to mention medication, does not necessarily produce one's best work.

Some writers have been able to withdraw from the desk gracefully, with or without regret: Samuel Beckett, Robert Graves and others wrote little in their latter years. For some, however, the thought that they are no longer able to do the thing that matters most to them is too much to bear. Ernest Hemingway took the most terrible way out, with a shot-gun. To the vast majority of those I have spoken with, the idea of ceasing to write altogether seems about as attractive a proposition as ceasing to eat or sleep.

How then can a writer who is still in his middle years, presume to offer advice to those older than himself? Of course I cannot; I offer the fruits of my experience and that of others, and trust, as usual, to my imagination. Becoming a mature writer may bring unimagined difficulties, but then, so does every other stage of one's writing life. The distinguished Canadian novelist Margaret Atwood speaks of an older writer's recurrent nightmare, in which all she is producing are rolls and rolls of white paper with nothing on them. Can any writer ever be satisfied with their lifetime's output? To paraphrase Dylan Thomas, before looking far ahead towards the good night and wondering how gently we shall go into it, perhaps we should glance at some of the pitfalls facing writers late in life, and seek ways by which we might skirt around them.

The Burned-out Writer

In a scene from Edward Bond's celebrated play *Bingo*, Ben Jonson asks the ageing William Shakespeare over a drink in a tavern, why he has not written anything of late. The question arises, as to whether he is written out, to which Shakespeare replies in the affirmative – he has nothing to say any more. Whether Shakespeare really had become written out towards the end of his life, we shall never know; it is an interesting thought, for he certainly seems to have stopped writing when he finally left London and retired to his comfortable house in Stratford.

In fact, I have never met a writer who considered himself or herself burned out, or bereft of anything to say, but I am assured they do exist. Many of them are people who worked extremely hard, and probably quite fast, particularly in the areas of film, television, or perhaps popular fiction, and finally got tired. It is not hard to imagine that feeling, or the notion that, one day, you may simply run out of steam. The late Frank Muir used to describe the 'torture' of forcing himself to write, and the wonderful feeling of relief when it was over once again. Hence the importance, as discussed in earlier chapters, of trying to pace oneself and of avoiding the temptation to do too much at once. For a lucky percentage of writers, the magic keeps working indefinitely, but for others it gets harder and harder to go back to the desk and create. For some, there comes a time when, like gunfighters of the Old West, they no longer have the stomach for the struggle. What then, is to be done? The options would seem to be starkly simple: one either hangs up the typewriter and retires to the rocking-chair, or gets back into the saddle and rides on. Understandably, some might want to look back over their lives, which for writers, leads to an obvious course of action.

Writing your Autobiography

Opinions divide sharply when it comes to autobiographies. Some swear they would never stoop so low, others have been happy to tell their life-stories in print, warts and all. Clearly it is something that a writer might want to think about, with the wisdom of hindsight to rely on, as well as the fact that the older one gets, the smaller the number of people who are still around to sue for libel.

Considering the fact that they are better equipped to do so than those in other walks of life, surprisingly few established writers have written autobiographies. Many are naturally diffident, modest people who have no wish to be remembered for anything other than their writings; or perhaps in some cases they were hoping that someone else would come along and save them the trouble. This seems a pity, because here is the ideal retirement pastime, and one that can take as long as you wish. You can keep inquisitive friends and relatives at bay for years by simply telling them that you are working on the autobiography, for there are always facts to be verified, letters to be written asking for reminiscences, and permission to be sought for inclusion of published material. Such things can take an eternity and need not be acted upon even when answers are received. All of this is particularly useful if you do not, in fact, want the thing to be published at all, in which case you will take steps to prevent some well-meaning friend, relative, or admirer from coming along and completing it after your death. Better to burn the manuscript while you can, then pretend it has been lost or stolen. No one will believe you, but what can they do about it?

Other Sorts of Writing

Older writers who are no longer too concerned about making an income from their work, may want to consider doing things that they enjoy and which still enable them to keep their hand in.

Charities

Local charities or charity shops may need the services of a writer from time to time for a range of things, from correspondence, or publicity material, to editing and writing newsletters (unpaid, of course). You can simply go along and offer your help.

Local Press

Publications in your area, from church magazines to the weekly newspaper, may also need your services. Of course, if you end up writing a column or contributing regularly to any publication except one that is distributed free of charge, you should be paid a reasonable rate for the job. Consult a handbook regarding current journalistic rates, or negotiate a mutually acceptable fee. Writing for a local magazine or newsletter is a pleasant way of keeping in touch with the world at large, as well as using your skills and experience. Some periodicals may even want to consider having a senior citizen correspondent who can cover the problems as well as the pleasures of the older members of the community. If gardening has become your pastime, there is always a healthy market for articles in this area. It cannot hurt to do some research, and then make an approach by letter or in person.

Letters

Writing letters regularly is a satisfying activity, in which you probably indulge in any case. I still correspond occasionally with writers I have not seen for years, and in some cases am unlikely to see again. When writing to them, I find I can give free rein to the pen and talk openly about matters that I would not share with others; being fellow-scribes, they understand one's concerns and thought processes, and reply in similar vein. I also enjoy composing the occasional letter of complaint about some item or service that I, or

SP have found unsatisfactory. While few would want to adopt the techniques of the Victor Meldrew school of communication, using one's writing skills here often brings rewards; the recipients, whether they be retailers, restaurateurs, or railway officials, seldom receive letters that are the least bit literary, let alone entertaining, and they may respond in charitable vein. It is also quite easy to get letters published, and a well-composed, topical missive that adds something to a current debate may well find its way on to the letters page of your national daily paper, while the local press may readily print anything that is lucid and interesting. Hence your name will appear in print, reminding those far and wide that you are still wielding the pen to good effect.

All of the above may of course seem trivial or incidental to you. Now that you are not (I hope) under the same pressure that you once were to earn your daily bread, and assuming you still retain your skills, you may think that it is now time to embark on your *magnum opus*, the definitive work of your generation, if not your era, that will draw on a life rich in memories, wisdom and experience. I do not scoff; I say do it. Even if it never gets finished, it is an admirable way to go out while you are still in the saddle. And if it does get finished you will have more than earned the right to sit back and enjoy a little peace.

The Little Place in France: Writers in Exile

In earlier (and cheaper) times, a large number of writers left our shores to spend their days in more exotic surroundings, often never to return. Noel Coward, with impeccable style and timing to the very last, died in his chair on the terrace one fine night, looking out over the sea from his house in Jamaica. Graham Greene, like many others, chose the South of France; Robert Graves, known to locals as 'Don Roberto', ended his days at Deya in Majorca, now a well-known tourist spot. Of course in recent years, and now with the ease of movement between EC countries, it has become possible for anyone to contemplate selling up and settling in warmer and sunnier climes, and many do. It is no longer a fantasy. At time of writing a lot of properties are cheaper in France and Spain than in the UK. European laws are becoming increasingly homogenized, and pensions are payable wherever you live. You can hire a removal van in England, ferry your belongings to your new home in the Dordogne or Catalonia, and drop the van in at the nearest compatible depot.

However, we are not merely talking here about retirement, for as we know, writers seldom retire. They may slow down, or change homes, but walk around the new place and you will always find a desk somewhere, with some work-in-progress lying on it. In fact writers have a long history of working in exile, and many have extolled the benefits of the objective distance it brings. From Ibsen and Henry James, via Joseph Conrad, James Joyce and Samuel Beckett, to Doris Lessing, this is a noble tradition, and it is probably as prevalent as it ever was, viz. the number of American writers working in London, and the Brits who make their homes in almost every corner of the world.

If the idea of moving abroad attracts you – and you need not be nearing retirement age to contemplate it – there are many factors to bear in mind aside from the obvious practicalities and logistics of finding somewhere to live, arranging financial and legal matters, and physically moving. These thing are not peculiar to writers and we do not have time to deal with them here. You may find books like *Living Abroad*, by Ingemar Torbiorn, or *The Daily Telegraph Guide to Living Abroad* by Michael Furnell useful.

What is peculiar to writers is their unique way of earning a living, and the question that arises is how best to continue it from outside one's native shores. Clearly those who work in the script-based fields of radio, theatre, or television, would be considerably disadvantaged by removing themselves not only from the source of commissions, but from the whole process. Personal contact is important in these areas, whether it means attending script and development meetings, rehearsals, or recordings. The writer usually needs to be around, and if he or she never appears, their input is lost and decisions will be taken in their absence. This could result in finished performances that do not meet the writer's expectations, or even their average standards, and reputations are damaged as a result. Not only that, if you do not travel to the UK from time to time, or make yourself available, you will slip further and further down people's lists of possible names when a project is first mooted. An agent may, of course, be able to do a great deal in terms of keeping your name afloat, but sooner or later the time will come when someone will say 'so-and-so's here in London, so we'll meet with him instead'.

For novelists and most of those who write books, it is far easier to operate from abroad. The cost of mailing and telephone calls is, of course, higher, but there are benefits which offset these expenses (smaller heating bills, perhaps), and with the Internet and e-mail it is becomingly increasingly less important where one happens to be based. Agents and publishers will not be overly concerned if they do not see you from one year to the next, provided you keep in touch by other means, and provided your work does not suffer from your living overseas.

I mentioned objective distance and indeed, some well-known writers found it easier to write about their native land by being outside it. Ibsen wrote his great plays, including *A Doll's House* and *Hedda Gabler* while living in exile in Rome, Dresden and Munich, though they were always set in his native Norway. James Joyce is another famous example, but let us not forget that in the course of writing a work like *Ulysses* he wrote home frequently, asking friends for, among other things, topographic details of Dublin that he was unable to verify for himself. The longer one lives abroad, the more out of touch one becomes with the life of one's country. If your novels are set in the here-and-now this can pose problems, not just with regard to everyday things like the layout of cities, or whether a certain bus service still operates, but more importantly with regard to language. As someone with a relative who has lived in Italy since 1980, I am frequently struck by the English she employs in her letters. It is old-fashioned, not merely in the general sense but quite specifically; the colloquialisms and idioms are those of the early Thatcher years, not of the Blairite *fin de siècle*.

For a well-established writer with a distinctive style, moving abroad is unlikely to present any serious difficulty. Presumably one carries on doing what one has always done. It is still advisable to keep, if not a foot in the old country, then some channels of communication open. Correspondence with friends and relatives back home will probably happen anyway, but it is just as important to maintain subscriptions to newspapers and periodicals, which can be mailed to you for the normal cost plus relevant postage. Reading is vital, but conversation with fellow-countrypeople is equally important. Spoken language changes from year to year, sometimes strikingly. When I was a schoolboy in the 1950s and early 1960s some of the French teachers I knew had never set foot in France, even though it was assumed that they spoke the language fluently. It was not until much later that I realized not only how appalling their accents were, but how stiff and old-fashioned their French was. It was as if an English tutor in France were basing his teaching on Dickens and Hardy. Nowadays anyone who teaches a foreign language will not only have completed part of their education in the relevant country, they will be expected to visit it at least once a year, to keep their language fresh and alive.

In the end, of course, where you live matters less than whether you are still able to write at your best, and if the surroundings are more to your liking, you will probably do good work in any case. Living in Corfu was the making of Gerald Durrell as a writer, and who could imagine Kipling without thinking of India? But living in a particular location, no matter how beautiful or exotic, does not mean one has to describe it; many writers simply need to leave their roots behind in order to write freely about them.

However, a well-known pitfall exists when moving abroad, even if only temporarily; if you are content to enjoy your new surroundings, to mingle with the locals, to sit in the shade and contemplate the beautiful scenery, you may get little or no writing done. This happened to someone I knew who settled on the unspoiled north-west coast of Majorca in the 1960s. The view from his villa was so breathtaking, he sat staring at it every day instead of writing (remarkably, the same thing happened to some of the painters who had moved there). Even meeting Robert Graves, who lived nearby, did not help; Graves knew how to turn away from the view and get on with his work. Of course this can, in theory, happen to you anywhere. The attractive south-western corner of England which I inhabit has long been populated by a disproportionate number of writers and artists, many of them originally from cities. One needs to be honest and face the real question: are you moving away in order to write, or simply to escape – and if so, to escape from what? For writers, as we know, carry their tools and materials with them wherever they go, and when you sit down once again at the desk in its new location, you face the same difficulties that you've always faced. What to write?

So here you are, on another part of this small, windy planet, under the same pale, insignificant sun, even if it does feel warmer. You may as well get on and make the best of it.

It does no harm, I believe, to finish on a philosophical note. Looking back over a writing life ought to bring, along with some natural frustration, a degree of contentment. Granted, you were unable to equal the masters, the ones who may have spurred you to write in the first place; no doubt they felt the same about their own particular heroes and mentors. We will always stand in the shadow of the great writers; one does what one can. On the other hand, you have made a difference of sorts, left behind you some original work, whether in print, on tape, or on celluloid, that did not exist before you created it, and yes, it will be there after you have gone, perhaps for longer than you expect. Some student in the year 2138, doing their PhD thesis on late twentieth-century popular culture, will be viewing restored copies of works which, at the time, you never expected to do more than pay the mortgage. Who knows how things will develop? Residents of a lunar settlement may turn away from their own breathtaking views, close the shutters and settle down with a reprinted, lightweight copy of your one bestseller.

When the reclusive, 75-year-old playwright Jean Genet was interviewed in the last year of his life, he was asked how he spent his time. With a shrug he quoted Saint Augustine, whom he described as a free spirit like himself: 'J'attends la mort' ('I wait for death.').

I hope that before I finally settle back to do the same I will have just begun a new piece of work, which will remain unfinished. That way, nobody will be able to say that I might not have done better, had I survived a little longer.

Appendix

Tax and Employment

The Department of Employment and Education draws a clear distinction between being unemployed and being non-employed. Being unemployed means that you are jobless, and assumed to be seeking work; being non-employed means that you have chosen to have no regular work for the moment; for example, you are living on savings, travelling, or taking a break between jobs. If you are registered as unemployed, the Government pays (or rather, credits) your national insurance contributions. If you are non-employed you are responsible for paying them yourself.

If you decide to become self-employed, contact your local Inland Revenue office and inform the Inspector of Taxes. Complete form CWF 1 – Notification of Self-employment – and you will be issued with a schedule D number. This means that you will be liable for self-assessment, and will receive a lengthy tax return form, plus supporting booklets and documentation (the whole as weighty as a road atlas though less interesting) around the end of the financial year. In fact this forbidding-looking form is not as difficult to fill in as you may fear, and there are helpline numbers for the confused. You may wish to obtain the handy guide *Coping with Self-assessment* by John Whiteley.

Being self-employed means that you will be liable to pay class 2 national insurance contributions (currently £6.55 per week), and an additional contribution, Class 4 NIC, if your income is greater than a certain amount which is based on a percentage of annual profits, the level being set each year by the Chancellor in the budget.

However, if your earnings are very low, you may be able to claim exemption, in which case you will be issued with a Certificate of Exception, CF 17. See also the Inland Revenue's booklet CWL 2, 'National Insurance Contributions for Self-employed People; Class 2 and Class 4' (available from any tax office).

If you remain in normal part-time or full-time employment and write in your spare time, any earnings you make from writing are, of course, liable to be taxed. Small amounts spread over long periods are unlikely to be of great concern to the tax inspector, but bear in mind that official bodies like the BBC make annual declarations to the Inland Revenue of the amounts they have paid to authors. For fuller, up-to-date guidelines see 'Tax and the Writer' in *The Writer's Handbook* and the section on finance in the *Writers' & Artists' Yearbook*, as well as the 'Quick Guides' published by the Society of Authors.

As a self-employed person you can claim for a range of business expenses to set against your income; the difference is your net profit for your accounting year, which need not follow the financial year. You are, in effect, a one-person business, and it is therefore essential to keep full and clear records of all income and expenditure. The simplest means of bookkeeping is to buy a hardbacked, ruled account book and use a double-entry system, i.e. one page for incomings and the facing page for outgoings. Each entry should be dated and supported by some documentation, which you can keep clipped together or filed. If you have received a cheque for a piece of work with no statement or remittance advice accompanying it, then photocopy the cheque and note the date it was received. All expenses must similarly be accompanied by a receipt of some kind. The broad categories I have always used in preparing my annual revenue account are as follows:

Stationery and Postage: This includes everything from a pen, or notebook, to computer supplies (discs and print-ribbons), photocopying and binding. An estimate of your average weekly postage costs is acceptable but this should not appear excessive. The post office will give you a receipt for stamps if you ask for one, so better to buy large quantities at a time.

Travel: Keep petrol receipts, bus or rail tickets and note when and where you travelled. Naturally the journey must have relevance to your work.

Telephone: The business proportion of your household telephone bill is a vague area, depending on how many people live in your home. I claim fifty per cent of the household bill, which is probably an underestimate. Trying to claim too large a percentage may understandably arouse suspicion.

Subscriptions and Periodicals: Annual subscriptions to bodies like the Society of Authors or the Writers' Guild are legitimate expenses, as are any publications which are relevant to your writing. For example, I claim the cost of my weekly copy of *The Stage & Television Today*; my newsagent totals up the price of the year's copies for me on headed notepaper.

Use of Home as Office: This is another grey area. I claim twenty-five per cent of the year's household bills for heating, lighting and insurance as being for business use. However, if you delineate part of your home (for example your study) purely for business purposes you may be liable for capital gains tax if you sell. It may be better to state that you work in various rooms at different times, or that you also use the study for other purposes such as paying bills.

Sundries: This can include various items such as bank charges and even theatre tickets, if visiting a particular performance was necessary to your work (as it has often been for me). A little common sense is needed; unrealistic amounts for seemingly trivial items will only incur suspicion.

There are other areas in which you can claim expenses, such as capital equipment (the cost of which may be carried over to the following year, if you prefer), research fees, accountancy fees, training and conference fees, etc., etc. If you are new to all of this and are unsure or uneasy about how to proceed, it may be best to consult an accountant for advice, at least initially. Once you get into the habit of keeping receipts and records, however, it will become second nature.

VAT

If your business turnover exceeds the set threshold (currently £51,000 in any twelve-month period), you are obliged by law to register for value added tax. Contact the nearest office of HM Customs & Excise, who will tell you how to register. You will be given a VAT number, and advice on how to make your quarterly returns. This is another complex area, and if you expect to earn this level of income it may well be worth securing the services of an accountant – you should be able to afford to do so.

Copyright

Copyright law in this country is complex. Very broadly speaking, you own the copyright to everything you write and nobody may make use of it in any way without your permission. However, proving that you are the author can be surprisingly difficult, and writers have resorted to devices such as registering a copy of their manuscript with a solicitor or notary. While no one of any integrity would knowingly steal a writer's work, it has happened.

In the busy world of television in particular, writers have been accused of plagiarizing other writers' ideas and plots, if not their dialogue. Unfortunately it is not possible to copyright an idea: anyone can claim they had already thought of a series set in, say, a rural country medical practice, and may even produce notes to prove it, which predate the plaintiff's initial proposal. Duplication is inevitable in today's television and film industries. Such disputes, in fact, seldom come to court: it is all very expensive and fraught with difficulties which most writers would rather avoid, even if they know they are in the right.

Conversely, you may not use anyone else's written work without first obtaining their permission, ideally their written permission, unless they have been dead for seventy years, or if seventy years have passed since date of first publication if posthumous, in which case they are usually deemed to be out of copyright (the limit used to be fifty years, but people live longer nowadays and the law was

at book sales, often for less than £1. You may already be aware of sales that take place in your area (advertisements often appear in the local press), but if not, it is well worth looking around. You have to be prepared to arrive early, take time to browse and to dig in dark corners. While you are very unlikely to find a rare first edition nowadays, you may well pick up a reference book at a bargain price.

Bibliography

Reference

Amateur Theatre Yearbook, The, ed. Charles Vance (Platform Publications, 1997)

Beal, George, *The Independent Book of Anniversaries* (Headline, 1992)

Brewer's Dictionary of Phrase & Fable (Wordsworth Editions Ltd., 1993)

Chambers Biographical Dictionary, ed. Magnus Magnusson (Chambers Harrap, 1990)

Chronicle of Britain, The, ed. Henrietta Heald (Chronicle Communications Ltd., 1992)

Clark, John O.E., *Word Perfect* (Harrap, 1987)

The Concise Oxford Dictionary of Quotations, ed. Angela Partington (Oxford University Press, 1994)

Fergusson, Rosalind, *The Penguin Rhyming Dictionary* (Market House Books, 1985)

The Guinness Book of Answers, 10th edn (Guinness Publishing, 1995)

Harvey, Sir Paul, *The Concise Oxford Companion to English Literature,* ed. Margaret Drabble, 4th edn (Oxford University Press, 1990)

Hoffmann, Ann, *Research for Writers* (A & C Black, 1996).

Legat, Michael, *An Author's Guide to Publishing* (Robert Hale Ltd., 1982)

Partridge, Eric, *A Dictionary of the Underworld* (Routledge & Kegan Paul, 1968)

Partridge, Eric, *The Penguin Dictionary of Historical Slang* (Penguin, 1972)

Radford, E. & M.A., *The Encyclopaedia of Superstitions*, ed. & revised by Christina Hale (Hutchinson, 1961)

Roget's Thesaurus of English Words and Phrases, ed. Betty Kirkpatrick (Penguin, 1998)

Ruse, Christina & Marilyn Hopton, *The Cassell Dictionary of Literary and Language terms* (Cassell, 1992)

The Small Press Guide, 4th ed. (Writers' Bookshop, 1998)

Whitaker's Almanack (J. Whitaker & Sons Ltd., published annually)

Withycombe, E.G., *The Oxford Dictionary of English Christian Names* (Oxford University Press, 1977)

Writers' & Artists' Yearbook (A & C Black, published annually)

The Writer's Handbook, ed. Barry Turner (Macmillan, published annually)

Further Reading

Aiken, Joan, *The Way to Write for Children* (Elm Tree Books, 1982)

Amis, Martin, *The Information* (Flamingo, 1995)

Anderson, Brian, *Writing About Travel: How to Research, Write and Sell Travel Guides and Articles* (How To Books, 1998)

Andrews, Richard, *Writing a Musical* (Robert Hale Ltd., 1997)

Ash, William, *The Way to Write Radio Drama* (Elm Tree Books, 1985)

Bair, Deirdre, *Samuel Beckett: A Biography* (Vintage, 1978)

Barker, Juliet R.V., *The Brontës* (Weidenfeld & Nicolson, 1994)

Best Radio Plays of 1978–1992 (Eyre Methuen, 1979–1993)

Bond, Edward, *Bingo* (Methuen, 1974)

Brande, Dorothea, *Becoming a Writer* (Macmillan, 1983)

Cleese, John & Connie Booth, *The Complete Fawlty Towers Comedy Scripts* (Methuen/Mandarin, 1988)

Cook, Judith, *Daphne: A Portrait of Daphne du Maurier* (Charnwood, 1992)

Cook, Judith, *Priestley* (Bloomsbury, 1997)

Cookman, Lesley, *Writing a Pantomime* (How To Books, 1999)

Crosland, Margaret, *Sade's Wife* (Peter Owen, 1995)

de Gale, Ann, *Writing for the Teenage Market* (A & C Black, 1993)

Dick, Jill, *Writing for Magazines* (A & C Black, 1994)

Dick, Jill, *Freelance Writing for Newspapers*, 2nd edn (A & C Black, 1998)

Ellmann, Richard, *James Joyce* (Oxford University Press, 1982)

Evans, Colin Haydn, *Writing for Radio* (Allison & Busby, 1991)

Furnell, Michael, *Daily Telegraph Guide to Living Abroad* (Kogan Page Ltd., 1994)

Golzen, Godfrey, *Working for Yourself: The Daily Telegraph Guide to Self-employment* (Kogan Page Ltd., 1995)

Gooch, Steve, Writing a Play (A & C Black, 1988)

Grant-Adamson, Lesley, *Teach Yourself Writing Crime and Suspense Fiction* (Hodder Headline, 1996)

Hemingway, Ernest, *A Moveable Feast* (Jonathan Cape, 1964)

Holmes, Richard, *Shelley: The Pursuit* (Weidenfeld & Nicolson, 1974)

Holroyd, Michael, *Bernard Shaw* (Chatto & Windus, 1997)

How to Write and Illustrate Children's Books and Get Them Published, eds. Treld Pelkey Bicknell & Felicity Trotman (Macdonald & Co., 1988)

Jellicoe, Ann, *Community Plays: How to Put Them On* (Methuen, 1987)

Jordan, Louise, *How to Write for Children and Get Published* (Piatkus Books, 1999)

LeFanu, Sarah, *Writing Fantasy Fiction* (A & C Black, 1996)

Legat, Michael, *How to Write Non-fiction* (Robert Hale Ltd., 1993)

Letters to An Actress: The Story of Turgenev and Savina, ed & translated by Nora Gottleib & Raymond Chapman (Allison & Busby, 1973)

MacShane, Frank, *The Life of Raymond Chandler* (Jonathan Cape, 1976)

McWhinnie. Donald, *The Art of Radio* (Faber, 1959)

Marks, Guy, *Travel Writing and Photography: All You Need to Make It Pay* (Traveller's Press 1997)

Medical Murders, ed. Jonathan Goodman (Piatkus Books, 1991)

Miller, Arthur, *Timebends: A Life* (Methuen, 1987)

Motion, Andrew, *Philip Larkin: A Writer's Life* (Methuen, 1982)

155

Obituaries from The Times, 1971–75 (Newspaper Archive Developments, 1978)

Phillipson, Ian, *How to Work from Home* (How To Books, 1992)

Polti, Georges, *The Thirty-six Dramatic Situations* (*The Writer*, Boston, Massachusetts, 1977)

Shay, Helen, *Copyright & Law for Writers* (How To Books, 1996)

Smethurst, William, *How to Write for Television,* 2nd edn (How To Books, 1998)

Thomson, Peter, *Shakespeare's Professional Career* (Cambridge University Press, 1992)

Torbiorn, Ingemar, *Living Abroad* (John Wiley & Sons Ltd., 1982)

Whiteley, John, *Coping with Self-assessment* (How To Books, 1997)

Wilde, Oscar, *Plays, Prose Writings and Poems* (Everyman, 1975)

Wolfe, Ronald, *Writing Comedy* (Robert Hale Ltd., 1992)

Wolff, Jurgen, *Successful Script Writing* (Writer's Digest Books, 1988)

Addresses

Arts Councils

Arts Council of England, 14 Great Peter Street, London SW1P
3NQ, Tel. 0171 333 0100.

Arts Council of Northern Ireland, MacNeice House, 77 Malone
Road, Belfast BT9 6AQ, Tel. 01232 385 200.

Arts Council of Wales, Holst House, 9 Museum Place, Cardiff CF1
3NX, Tel. 01222 394 711.

Republic of Ireland Arts Council, 70 Merrion Square, Dublin 2,
Republic of Ireland, Tel. (01) 661 1840.

Scottish Arts Council, 12 Manor Place, Edinburgh EH3 7DD, Tel.
0131 226 6051.

Regional Arts Boards

Eastern Arts Board, Cherry Hinton Hall, Cherry Hinton Road,
Cambridge CB1 4DW, Tel. 01223 215 355.

East Midlands Arts Board, Mountfields House, Epinal Way,
Loughborough, Leicestershire LE11 0QE, Tel. 01509 218 292.

London Arts Board, Elme House, 133 Long Acre, London WC2E
9AF, Tel. 0171 240 1313.

Northern Arts Board, 9–10 Osborne Terrace, Jesmond, Newcastle
upon Tyne NE2 1NZ, Tel. 0191 281 6334.

North West Arts Board, Manchester House, 22 Bridge Street,
Manchester M3 3AB, Tel. 0161 834 6644.

South East Arts Board, Union House, Eridge Road, Tunbridge
Wells, Kent TN4 8HF, Tel. 01892 507 200.

Southern Arts Board, 13 St Clement Street, Winchester, Hants SO23
9DQ, Tel. 01962 855 099.

South West Arts Board, Bradninch Place, Gandy Street, Exeter EX4 3LS, Tel. 01392 218 188.

West Midlands Arts Board, 82 Granville Street, Birmingham B1 2LH, Tel. 0121 631 3121.

Yorkshire & Humberside Arts Board, 21 Bond Street, Dewsbury, West Yorkshire WF13 1AX, Tel. 01924 455 555.

Television and Radio

BBC Television, Television Centre, Wood Lane, London W12 7RJ, Tel. 0181 743 8000.

BBC Radio, Broadcasting House, London W1A 1AA, Tel. 0171 580 4468.

BBC Midlands & East, Broadcasting Centre, Pebble Mill Road, Birmingham B5 7QQ, Tel. 0121 414 8888.

BBC North, New Broadcasting House, Oxford Road, Manchester M60 1SJ, Tel. 0161 200 0200.

BBC South, Broadcasting House, Whiteladies Road, Bristol, Avon BS8 2LR, Tel. 0117 973 2211.

BBC Scotland, Broadcasting House, Queen Margaret Drive, Glasgow G12 8DG, Tel. 0141 339 8844.

BBC Northern Ireland, Broadcasting House, 25–27 Ormeau Avenue, Belfast BT2 8HQ; Tel. 01232 338 000.

BBC Wales, Broadcasting House, Llandaff, Cardiff CF5 2YQ, Tel. 01222 572 888.

Theatres

The following is an up-to-date listing (1999) of theatres that are willing to read unsolicited scripts. It is not exhaustive but represents, in the author's view, the best range of options for the new writer at the present time.

Birmingham Repertory Theatre, Broad Street, Birmingham B1 2EP, Tel. 0121 236 6771. Literary Manger: Ben Payne.

The Bush Theatre, Shepherds Bush Green, London W12 8QD, Tel. 0171 602 3703. Literary Manager: Tim Fountain.

Hampstead Theatre, Swiss Cottage Centre, Avenue Road, London NW3 3EX, Tel. 0171 722 9224. Literary Manager: Ben Jancovich.

Paines Plough – New Writing Theatre, 4th Floor, 43 Aldwych, London WC2B 4DA, Tel. 0171 240 4533. Literary Development Manager: Mark Ravenhill.

Royal Court Theatre, St Martins Lane, London WC2N 4BG, Tel. 0171 565 5050. Literary Manager: Graham Whybrow.

Royal Exchange Theatre Company, St Ann's Square, Manchester M2 7DH, Tel. 0161 833 9333. Literary Manager: Sarah Frankcom.

Royal National Theatre, South Bank, London SE1 9PX, Tel. 0171 928 2033. Literary Manager: Jack Bradley.

Soho Theatre Company, 21 Dean Street, London W1V 6NE, Tel. 0171 287 5060. Literary Manager: Paul Sirett.

Theatre Royal Stratford East, Gerry Raffles Square, London E15 1BN, Tel. 0181 534 7374. Literary Manager: Rita Mishra.

West Yorkshire Playhouse, Playhouse Square, Leeds, West Yorkshire LS2 7UP, Tel. 0113 244 2141. Literary Co-ordinator: Lucy Best.

Other Useful Addresses

Authors Licensing & Collecting Society, Marlborough Court, 14–18 Holborn, London EC1N 2LE, Tel. 0171 395 0600.

The Arvon Foundation:

1 Lumb Bank, Heptonstall, Hebden Bridge, West Yorks HX7 6DF, Tel. 01422 843 7147.

2 Totleigh Barton, Sheepwash, Beaworthy, Devon EX21 5NS, Tel. 01409 231 338.

3 Moniack Mhor, Teavarran, Kiltarlity, Beauly, Inverness-shire IV4 7HT, Tel. 01463 741 675.

New Playwrights' Trust, Interchange Studios, 15 Dalby Street, London NW5 3NQ, Tel. 0171 284 2818.

The Poetry Society, 22 Betterton Street, London WC2H 9BU, Tel. 0171 420 9880.

Society of Authors, 84 Drayton Gardens, London SW10 9SB, Tel. 0171 373 6642.

Spotlight Casting Directory & Contacts, 7 Leicester Place, London WC2H 7BP.

Women Writers Network, 23 Prospect Road, London NW2 2JU, Tel. 0171 794 5861.

Writers in Prison Network, 17 Upper Lloyd Street, Rusholme, Manchester M14 4HY.

Writers' Guild of Great Britain, 430 Edgware Road, London W2 1EH, Tel. 0171 723 8074.

Inland Revenue, National Insurance Contributions Office, Self-employment Group, Newcastle upon Tyne NE98 1YX, Tel. 0645 154 655.

Locomotive Software, 10 Vincent Works, Dorking RH4 3HJ, Tel. 01306 747 757.

The Screenwriter's Store, 10 Moor Street, Soho, London W1V 5LJ, Tel. 0171 287 9009, Fax. 0171 287 6009.